S0-BCS-331

# SLOWING DOWN
# TO THE SPEED OF *Love*

# SLOWING DOWN
# TO THE SPEED OF *L*OVE

*How to Create a Deeper, More Fulfilling Relationship*

*in a Hurried World*

JOSEPH BAILEY, M.A., L.P.

**McGraw·Hill**

New York   Chicago   San Francisco   Lisbon   London   Madrid   Mexico City
Milan   New Delhi   San Juan   Seoul   Singapore   Sydney   Toronto

**Library of Congress Cataloging-in-Publication Data**

Bailey, Joseph V.
    Slowing down to the speed of love : how to create a deeper, more fulfilling relationship in a hurried world / Joseph Bailey.
        p.    cm.
    Includes bibliographical references and index.
    ISBN 0-07-140249-7 (hardcover) — ISBN 0-07-143873-4 (paperback)
    1. Love—Psychological aspects.    2. Man-woman relationships.
3. Quality of life.    4. Lifestyles.    5. Simplicity.    I. Title.

HQ801 .B124    2003
306.7—dc21                            2002073683

Copyright © 2003 by Joseph Bailey. All rights reserved. Printed in the United States of America. Except as permitted under the United States Copyright Act of 1976, no part of this publication may be reproduced or distributed in any form or by any means, or stored in a database or retrieval system, without the prior written permission of the publisher.

1 2 3 4 5 6 7 8 9 0   FGR/FGR   3 2 1 0 9 8 7 6 5 4

ISBN 0-07-140249-7 (hardcover)
ISBN 0-07-143873-4 (paperback)

Interior design by Monica Baziuk

McGraw-Hill books are available at special quantity discounts to use as premiums and sales promotions, or for use in corporate training programs. For more information, please write to the Director of Special Sales, Professional Publishing, McGraw-Hill, Two Penn Plaza, New York, NY 10121-2298. Or contact your local bookstore.

This book is printed on acid-free paper.

*To My True Love, Wife, and Spiritual Partner, Michael*

∞

# CONTENTS

⟨⟨∘——∘⟩⟩

CONTENTS

# FOREWORD

As an author, one of the greatest honors I can think of is to write the foreword to a book that I believe will help many people. This is one of those books and this is one of those honors. Before I introduce you to the book, however, please allow me to say a few words to you about the author.

I have a stone in my backyard with some words etched on it that come from Mahatma Gandhi. He said, "My life is my message." I've known Joe Bailey for many years, and he is someone who falls into this category. He is kind, patient, and insightful, and is an extremely good listener. When I'm around him, time seems to slow down. Some of the unnecessary urgency, as well as the frenzied pace of life, seem to disappear or at the very least calm down. My wife, Kris, and my two daughters feel the same way. To all of us, as well as to so many others who know Joe, his life is his message.

Joe and his wife, Michael, have one of the most beautiful relationships I've ever seen—which is one of the reasons I'm so interested in what he has to say. When I reflect on why this is true, it strikes me that both Joe and Michael are extremely "present." Each has slowed down to the speed of love, and they make you feel like the most important person in their lives—in that moment. They each have the capacity to be "right there" with you, which makes you feel connected, centered, and loved. In their relationship together, they have a deep mutual respect for one another and are obviously very much in love. They are both at ease with themselves and with each other as a couple. They have tapped that place inside themselves where love is always present.

*Slowing Down to the Speed of Love* will help you access that same place within you. Unlike so many other books, it doesn't offer artificial techniques but rather a road map to help you discover, or in many instances rediscover, your own source of inner wisdom and a genuine sense of ease. When you quiet down and are in contact with your own inner intelligence, some nice things begin to happen to your life and to your relationships. You become less defensive and reactive. Forgiveness becomes easy and effortless. You are able to maintain a lighthearted way of being, and you can see the innocence in others.

When you slow down to the speed of love you become more connected with others, particularly those you love. Your presence becomes deeper, and your ability and willingness to listen become more natural and effective. It's one thing to say, "It's important to be present or in the moment," and it's something else to experience what that really means. For me, this book has had the effect of turning the concept of being present into more of an actual experience. It helped me understand the difference between what I have sometimes thought of as "love" and a deeper, more timeless, and unshakable version. The deeper love Bailey writes about isn't contingent upon getting what we want from our relationships but rather from connecting to a deeper source within us so that our relationships will become what we want. It's actually the opposite of the way many of us have approached love in our lives. The idea is that as you, yourself, become more peaceful and loving, these qualities will show up in your relationships. It's also the case that as you tap into that place in yourself where love is ever present, you are better able to "draw" out that love in others.

One of my favorite aspects to this book is that, when reading it, it becomes obvious that what Bailey is saying is remarkably simple. He's saying that love is, in fact, our most natural state. There isn't anything we really have to "do" to access love in our lives other than slow down and become present enough to feel and experience it. The image I think of is getting out of our own way so that the love that is already there has a chance to surface. And once it does, our relationships with others become easier—and more loving. They have a chance to fall into place as our frustrations are replaced by wisdom.

*Slowing Down to the Speed of Love* is more than just an interesting read. I believe it has the capacity to touch something inside you—deep enough to help you make significant positive changes in your life. I encourage you to not think about it as much as to absorb the material. As you reflect upon, as opposed to study, the wisdom of these pages, I hope you'll connect with the most loving part of yourself.

∞

DR. RICHARD CARLSON
Author of *Don't Sweat the Small Stuff*
May 2002

# ACKNOWLEDGMENTS

THIS BOOK has truly been a labor of love, done in relationship with many dear friends, professional colleagues, and family. Writing *Slowing Down to the Speed of Love* has felt synergistic, with many people helping me directly and indirectly. It has been as though many forces, within and without, have guided me to weave the concepts and ideas of this book into a fabric of understanding timeless love.

It is difficult to know where to begin to thank so many who have aided in the writing of this book. I shall start with my true love and wife, Michael. We have been soul mates in the deepest sense. For twenty-two years, we have loved each other and grown continuously within ourselves and together. Michael has been a friend, teacher, lover, and editor. I couldn't have written this book without the inspiration I have felt from the love I have found with her. In writing *Slowing Down to the Speed of Love,* she has been my encourager, my challenger, and my "truth editor."

The second person to thank is my dear friend and agent, Mark Chimsky. I met Mark many years ago when he was my editor at Harper SanFrancisco. When he left Harper to pursue his own editorial business, I asked him to help me with my book proposal. Writing it under Mark's tutelage was like going back to graduate school to study English. I learned so much from him about the art of being a writer. I kept hoping Mark would represent me as my agent, but he only took on a few clients in this role. Eventually, Mark agreed to represent me. However, he has been more than a book agent—he has been a mentor, friend, advocate, and editor. He demands the highest quality of writing that I am capable of and will not let the writing go until it meets his standard. At times, I have felt impatient with his level of perfection, but it has forced me to grow as a writer. I feel so taken care of by Mark, and I feel very lucky to have him as my agent.

One of my greatest supporters and friends for many years has been Richard Carlson. He and I wrote *Slowing Down to the Speed of Life* in 1997, which served as a springboard for this book. I especially want to thank Richard for his kind words in the Foreword and for all his love and friendship throughout the years.

I want to thank my dear friend Lia Venchi, whose editorial comments and suggestions were immensely helpful. Her insights and support were a continual source of inspiration for my writing.

I want to express my gratitude to Laurie Viera, my personal editor, who understands my voice and brings it out more clearly with each of her edits. She has a gift of language, but retains the voice of integrity of the author.

I am grateful to Judith McCarthy, my editor at Contemporary Books/McGraw-Hill. Her enthusiasm for this project, her faith in the book, and her kind and intelligent manner have made me feel at home with my new publisher. I knew the first time I spoke with her on the phone that this was with whom I wanted to publish my book.

Lastly, I want to thank all those who have taught me to love—my parents, who loved each other so sweetly for sixty-three years; my son Ben and his family; and all my loving friends and family. I also want to thank all the couples whom I interviewed for this book. Their stories have inspired me and will move countless others who read them.

# SLOWING DOWN
## TO THE SPEED OF *Love*

# 1

# WHAT IS LOVE?

THIS IS A BOOK for our fast-paced, hectic times. If you have picked it up because you are wondering how to find time for intimacy in your fast-paced life, if your relationship has lost its luster and attraction, or if your to-do list has intruded on the quality of your life and your relationships, read on. It may sound unrealistic, but by realizing the principles that this book points to, you may be able to solve all these issues at once. Whether in a relationship, or hoping to discover new love, the solution to loving connections may be simpler than you think.

"You never have time to listen to me anymore!" "You don't really hear what I am saying to you." "You never have time for me!" "Why do I feel so disconnected from people? I have lots of relationships, yet I feel lonely." "I can't seem to find anyone who is 'right' for me. What's the matter with me?" "Does true love really exist?" "I love my mate, we just don't have time for each other anymore between work, raising kids, and all the other obligations of life."

Does any of this sound familiar? If so, you may be normal in our contemporary culture of frenzy, fast pace, and multitasking. In this new millennium, we are living our lives more and more in the fast lane, trying to juggle ten balls at once while walking across a tightrope and losing our inner balance in the process. As a result, the quality of our relationships is suffering. It is no wonder that 50 percent of all first and 60 percent of second marriages end in divorce. You might wonder if we have time for love and friendship anymore.

Most of us who are or who have been in committed relationships follow the typical path of being infatuated, falling in love, and then experiencing disappointment, hurt, anger, disillusionment, and inevitable pain. If you are at a crisis point and are reading this, you probably haven't given up hope, and you aren't alone in your struggle. Most couples eventually hit this wall. Even if you aren't in a crisis, you may just want more out of your relationship.

*Slowing Down to the Speed of Love* is about turning adversity and conflict into an opportunity for transformation, as well as rejuvenating an "average" relationship. These insights will also keep a new relationship on a loving track, and, if you're not currently in a relationship but would like to be, show you what true love is.

You may think that you have failed, that you were stupid to think your relationship could ever work in the first place, or that your partner is at fault. Don't be discouraged. You may not realize it, but you are on the brink of change and potential transformation. Crisis and conflict are ways of waking us up to the possibilities that lie dormant in any relationship. Have hope that if you gain the proper perspective and understanding, you can change this present difficult time into a turning point.

For the past twenty-eight years, I have been a couples therapist and seminar leader. I have written this book for all couples and singles who are struggling, as my wife and I did until we gained an understanding of how to have a healthy relationship. Looking over those years, the catalyst that moved my clients and me out of pain and insecurity and into a new understanding of our relationships and our true nature was *willingness*.

This transforming power is the willingness to be open, to discover who we are and how we can experience love in all of our relationships. It is the difference between choosing to continually move forward and experience more love in our lives and stopping out of fear of letting go of familiar ways of doing and thinking. All it takes is a little willingness. At times, you may feel that it takes courage to let go of the old and familiar; even if it is painful, the familiar can be comfortable. I can truthfully say that in light of what I know now, I would not want any of my old beliefs and habits back. As you read, just ask yourself along the way, "Am I willing to discover love that is timeless?"

My original insight into transforming relationships was triggered by the principles of inner peace and spiritual fulfillment known as *Health Realization*, which was inspired by Sydney Banks in the 1970s after he had a realization about the nature of the mind and human experience. *Slowing Down to the Speed of Love* is a road map to the principles that allow us to understand how life works and how to access our birthright of love and personal fulfillment.

Here is a story from a seminar participant (in her own words) that illustrates the possibility of change for all relationships.

### Allison and Justin's Story of Transformation

Justin and I met twenty-six years ago as colleagues in a youth outreach training program. We were involved in similar work with high school teens for two years, and during that time we became good friends. Gradually, our friendship turned into something much stronger.

We weren't just in love. We were hopelessly in love. After dating for two years, we married. The first seven years of married life were wonderful. We were soul mates and so happy to be together. But in our third year of marriage, we learned that Justin would be unable to parent biologically. We grieved deeply and then moved on, trusting that our lives would be full and rich without children.

After being married for seven years, both of us decided that we wanted to change jobs and remove ourselves from the intense way we had been involved in service to others. Changing careers and coming to terms with his infertility seemed to overwhelm Justin, and quickly and silently, he became depressed. For the next few years, it became really challenging for Justin and me to relate to each other and communicate effectively. For the first time, we felt alienated from each other and unable to get our emotional needs met. We separated for nine months during that time, and on some days the future of our relationship looked bleak indeed.

We eventually got back together and adopted two wonderful children. Although we experienced true joy in our family life, it wasn't consistent and Justin still struggled with depression. He worked to be there for our kids with whatever energy he had, yet he withdrew from me and was noncommunicative. I eventually became filled with resentment and anger that I was not living the life I wanted to live. We blamed each other for our misery and felt lost as to where to find help.

Over the course of several years, Justin saw several psychiatrists, therapists, and did an intensive regimen of drug therapy. On occasion, medication worked for a while, but nothing lasted for more than a few months. I participated in my own therapy, did what reading I could find on depression, but there was no relief in my marital situation.

I would become so enraged when I heard professionals tell Justin that he had dysthymia (a depressive mood disorder), along with frequent bouts of major depression, and that all he could do was try to manage it. It seemed as though his fate was cast. I knew deep in my heart that Justin could free himself from the inside out, but I was having trouble doing that effectively myself and felt trapped.

Depression wreaks incredible havoc on a marriage. I felt like a failure every single day, because although I was living life fully with my children, in my career, and in other aspects of my personal life, my inability to accept Justin and be at peace with his behavior and choices eroded my self-esteem something fierce.

As a last attempt, we saw a highly recommended marriage therapist whom I liked a great deal as a person. Yet she, too, did nothing to help us. I most often left the sessions feeling worse than when I walked in the door. Old wounds were reopened and relived. What good was that?

I began to contemplate divorce. Even though it was almost unthinkable, it seemed the only option. I wanted relief from Justin's darkness, moodiness, and silent brooding. His depression had become such an unruly monster in our lives. It got all the attention that I was starving for. I no longer liked myself and clearly had become part of the problem. Though I, too, became depressed, I knew there was a better way to live, and to stay stuck seemed destructive.

Then, Justin and I attended Joe Bailey's course in September 1999, where Joe taught us a whole new way of looking at our relationship by focusing on one moment at a time. Slowly we began to put aside the past. Looking back, even for a second, did nothing for me—for either of us. We both stayed in the moment, and the resentment disappeared. Resenting the past didn't serve me. Analyzing it was only wasted energy. Who cares what happened then? Who cares how long it went on? It was over, and I had no desire to return there.

We learned about deep listening. We learned about letting our thinking flow. We came to see that when we had negative thoughts about each other or life that they would pass. We began to take walks together again. We sought to enjoy each other, not fix, correct, blame, enlighten, or control each other. As a result, humor has reentered our lives. We laugh more easily. We no longer try to be right, but seek to be loving. Acceptance abounds. Affection has returned, and daring to trust is a part of our relationship once again.

Before we reached this understanding, depression had us by the throat. Regrettably, most of our other mental health professionals, though well-meaning, had done nothing to aid us. In this new model of therapy, I learned about innocence, which is such a freeing idea. It helped me to not judge Justin and to stop being angry with him. The principles we learned in Joe's seminar have taught us what nothing else could. We now live in joy, lightness, and happiness.

I had always known that I was meant to live fully, regardless of whatever was going on with Justin. I had, in many ways, built as good a life as I was able at the time. I worked for so much and got so much. And yet happiness had eluded me.

I can't say I ever desired calmness. I always thought I was too high-energy for calm. Yet what I've discovered is that when I have a calm mind and a calm heart, happiness settles on me like a butterfly. And happiness, like a butterfly, had eluded me for more than a decade. As we both calm our minds and use this framework to relate to each other, we are slowly healed day-by-day and grateful for each moment we have.

I am so happy that I did not pursue a divorce. I never wanted to break up our family. Now, we plan to practice the Health Realization principles a day at a time. We've done further reading on these ideas and trust, once again, in each other's innocence and goodness and love. Justin is now free of his depression and is off all medication. Our marriage was saved at the eleventh hour. And our kids, as well as Justin and I, are reaping the benefits!

Justin and Allison did several things that were markedly different from their previous attempts to deal with their marriage problems and Justin's depression. First, they learned that the source of our experience is in our power to think and make our thoughts conscious. We create all of our emotions, perceptions, and experiences through the principles of *Thought* and *Consciousness*. By realizing these first two principles, Justin and Allison understood that going back and analyzing their past was not only unhelpful, but it also kept breathing life into it, validating the past as if it were still a reality. Dwelling on the past would be as unhealthy as having the flu last week and then proceeding to relive it for days, weeks, and even months later through conversations and memories, thus reminding themselves unnecessarily of something that was long past. Yet millions of people who participate in conventional psychological practices are engaged in a similar rehashing of past events, emotions, and behaviors. These practices muddy the water of the present and keep people from experiencing the feelings of *timeless love*, which can only be felt in this moment.

Justin and Allison also learned about *deep listening*. They learned to hear each other, not through the contamination of past memories and habits, but through the pure filter of consciousness that exists in all of us when we are fully in the present moment. When they learned to be responsible for creating their own experience, they quit blaming each other for their own emotions and behavior. As a result, they transformed their emotions of anger and resentment into compassion and understanding.

As Justin and Allison each learned to tap into his or her true Self—which is the true source of timeless love—they realized that they already had the love they sought. They were able to stop searching for it in each other. When they quit expecting to be fulfilled from the outside, they experienced true fulfillment from the inside.

Fortunately, the couple in this story learned the principles that enabled them to reconnect with their love instead of breaking up, but often that isn't the case. Justin and Allison discovered the solution while already in a failing relationship, and they succeeded in salvaging it. To find the origin of what makes relationships fail, we must explore what we were initially searching for in it. Though we carry the elements for a healthy relationship within us, our lack of awareness of those elements sets ourselves up for failure before we even meet our mate.

In this next section I will share my own search for love and how it led to a great deal of pain and disappointment.

## My Own Search for Love

As a young man, I dreamed of finding my true love. Sometimes she would be 5 feet, 3 inches tall and would have blue eyes, blond hair, and a beautiful smile; at other times she had long dark hair and exotic features. And she would be madly in love with me, of course. Although my checklist for the perfect mate changed and evolved over time, I always had one. When I met someone who came close to my idea of perfection, I would mentally compare her traits to those on my list, though I was not always aware I was doing so.

I also had many beliefs about the way relationships should be. I thought it was *her* job to make me happy—to take away my emptiness, to make me laugh, to make me feel good about myself, to do the things a "good mate" should do. I had a lot of rules and expectations, most of which were never met.

Almost all of my relationships followed a predictable pattern of stages:

1. Attraction
2. Infatuation
3. Love
4. Expectations based on my past conditioning
5. Unfulfilled expectations
6. Doubt
7. Disappointment
8. Resentment
9. Anger
10. Disillusionment
11. Break-up

This pattern repeated itself numerous times.

I didn't seem to be alone in this process. Most of my friends experienced similar stages, and most of the songs I listened to spoke of similar quests for love. Naturally, I believed that this cycle of love and loss was just the way things were.

Eventually I got married and began the cycle again, but with two additional emotions—I felt trapped and guilty. My wife wasn't making me happy at all. In fact, she was making me very unhappy. She wasn't living up to my expectations of how she should be nurturing and anticipate my needs. I had only one recourse—to try to change her. Needless to say, she didn't exactly appreciate my efforts. So, we spent another seven years together trying to make it work—with lots of marriage counseling, soul searching, and arguments—and eventually came to the conclusion that we weren't meant for each other and we separated.

After my divorce, my quest for true love resumed, though I was a little more cautious, fearful, and mistrustful. Again, I fell in love several times, thinking I had found the right person, only to eventually become disillusioned. By age thirty-two, I was depressed, lonely, and had reached the conclusion that in the new age of liberation of the sexes, marriage and true love were not in the cards for me. I saw that others were having relationship problems too, and no one seemed to have the answers.

Ironically, I was a marriage counselor and a psychotherapist at the time, which made me feel doubly a failure. I thought that of all people, I should know how to have a successful relationship!

Though I had given up on some level, the yearning for true love continued inside me. I tried to squelch it, but to no avail. After I lost a relationship that I really thought was *the one*, I sank into a deep depression.

Ironically, my pain became a turning point in my search for love.

In my despair, I turned within. I asked God to heal me of my agony. A quiet voice inside whispered, "You already have what you seek.

Accept yourself fully as you are." That moment I had my first glimpse of what was to be a new phase of becoming who I truly am. From that small first step, I committed myself to uncovering the spiritual essence of my being that had been buried under my ego for most of my life. Although I wavered many times after that day and was unable to completely sustain the awareness contained in that insightful flash, my commitment to finding true inner love and happiness remained unshakable.

For many years I had heard this notion and even taught it to the individuals and couples who came to me for psychotherapy. However, I hadn't truly realized it for myself. Finally, I understood the real meaning of the first guideline to true love:

*You are enough. You are already whole. Don't look to another to fill what is already complete. You are love.*

I felt such relief! All the pressure to find the right person was suddenly gone. The pressure I had put on others to fulfill all my personal needs also disappeared to a great degree. The way I felt and behaved began to change. I was calm and more self-assured. I could just be me, and that was enough. I quit looking for love from others, from the outside. Instead, I fell in love with life! I felt love for everything and everyone that I saw. My experience of love was no longer contingent upon being loved back or getting my needs met. My neediness began to subside and was replaced by feelings of deep contentment. The bottomless hole that I had experienced all my life was no longer empty, so my need to fill it with love from another person was no longer necessary. This "knowing" that the source of love is within me and everyone was enough to sustain me through the times when I became entangled in my old way of thinking and lost sight of timeless love. I was beginning to glimpse another possibility—one that was not a struggle, one that was not bound by limitations. Instead, I intuitively knew I was ready for a new kind of love, one that was unconditional and timeless. I knew this, though I had not yet experienced it.

## Redefining Love

Now I'd like to set the stage by suggesting a new definition of love. I would like to talk about a love that is eternal, one that evolves and grows over time, a love that is *timeless*. In our ever-accelerating, fast-paced world, we don't seem to have enough time for each other—to listen, to share, and to connect. To experience this new kind of love, we must learn to stop time and live fully in the present. This is a paradigm shift—from the world of finite time and space to a world of infinite time with no boundaries.

Timeless love is quite different from the kind of love I'd spent much of my life searching for. Timeless love is born not of *my* needs, expectations, or desires, but is instead a spiritual love that is the essence of my spiritual nature. You may ask, "How can a love like this satisfy me? How can a love like this be experienced with another person?" Yet, most of us have experienced moments of this type of love, although fleetingly. At times, when we are undistracted by external events and our own mental juggling, expectations, and judgments—when time stands still and we are in the moment—we feel this kind of love. It is like the sun peeking out of the clouds after a month of November darkness. The sun was and always has been there, but it seems so rare. Lovers often speak of "time standing still." When we are in the moment and connected to this timeless feeling, we are filled up with an infinite supply of love.

The contrast to timeless love is what I call *time-bound love*, a conditional type that has expectations attached. Just fill in the blank for the expectation that sounds most familiar to you. "I'll love you if

_____" ("you love me first," "you make me happy," "you do what I expect," "you like what I like," "you believe what I believe," and so on). When we are involved in time-bound love, we often feel caught up in time—impatient, judgmental, anxious, unfulfilled, and needy.

Conditional love is essentially selfish. In my pursuit of time-bound love I tried to act loving, to act kind, to act like I was listening, but it was only a means to get what *I* wanted. For example, when I was young, if I wanted to receive a compliment about how I looked, I might compliment the other person, hoping that person would do the same. This type of interaction puts an expectation and pressure on the other person that, in turn, leads to tension and resentment.

This next story from one of my clients illustrates how trying to meet our time-bound, ego-based needs can lead to disappointment, hurt, and failed relationships.

### A Story of Time-Bound Love

Carey had a very low self-image. In high school she had suffered from anorexia, and in her young adult years she was on a perpetual diet.

When she met Brent, she fell head over heels in love with him. Not only did she think he was "really cute," but he was also quick to compliment her on her hair or a new outfit or how she looked in a bathing suit. As time went on, however, his compliments became less frequent, and she became very angry.

"How could I have ended up with such a selfish jerk?" she often thought to herself. He was no longer feeding her ego, and she was in withdrawal from her addiction to his compliments.

"Why don't you just grow up?" Brent blurted out one day. He was sick and tired of constantly having to nurture her fragile sense of self-worth.

Eventually, he threatened to end the relationship and she pleaded for him to come to couples counseling with her.

Through the process of Health Realization therapy, they both learned to look within for the source of their true happiness and love—timeless love. They realized that it wasn't up to another person to make them happy or miserable. They learned that their inner essence was a spiritual core that is experienced as a feeling of love. As a result of this realization, the constant tug-of-war for attention subsided and their love blossomed. By recognizing that the source of their unpleasant emotions was their own thinking, they were able to calm their rampant expectations and accept each other for who they truly were.

Time-bound love takes what the other person does very personally. "What did he mean by that statement?" we ask ourselves. "Why isn't she attracted to me tonight?" "Does he still love me?"

In self-centered, time-bound love, we are always interpreting *everything* the other person says or does. Every word and gesture is fraught with meaning of our own making. We are constantly busy thinking about the state of the relationship and how it is doing. "Is each of us contributing equally to the relationship?" "Is the ledger balanced?" "Does he do as much for the family and me as I do for him?" "Am I being taken advantage of?" Me, me, me, me, me. Self-absorbed love is all about me. It isn't really love at all.

## *Timeless Love*

Unlike the conditional, self-centered nature of time-bound love, timeless love is born of our spiritual nature and therefore has no personal needs. Timeless love is the only type that is permanent and of any real value. It is unconditional and non–ego based; it is effortless and natural. And it is transcendent, because it has nothing to do with me, me, me.

The essence of each of us is this divine source—love. When we are aware of our true nature, the importance of our individual ego-self fades. As we place less importance on our personality quirks, expectations, and neediness, we open ourselves to our true nature—love.

Love is the core of our being, so what could be easier and more natural than for our true, loving nature to flow in our lives and in our relationships? "Being" is life supported by the spiritual energy of all life—it is our true, natural Self. To *be* does not require effort; it just *is*—a natural way of being.

Note: It is a common practice to capitalize Self when used in the context of *true* Self, in order to distinguish the difference between the concept of a limited self and the concept of our unlimited spirit. In this book, I use the term *natural Self* interchangeably with the term *true Self.*

I know that when I am most relaxed, content, and peaceful, my life is easy. I am present; I am connected to people; I am love and compassion—I am alive. I never knew that in those moments I was experiencing my true, transcendent Self, not my ego-created personality. In such instances, my ego, with its likes, dislikes, defenses, and opinions, disappeared. It is now shocking to me that for all those years I had been confusing my ego and personality for my true Self.

Our true Self is who we *really* are; but we've had little experience or awareness of our innate, natural Self. We have more experience relating to our ego-personality—who we *think* we are. Early on we're all taught, by example, to define ourselves by our opinions and our beliefs. We unconsciously created an image of self-importance, our ego, and we thought ourselves to be separate from our spiritual source and from each other. Our true Self is unlearned; it is natural. When we are aware of who we truly are, it is unnecessary to figure out and label ourselves.

| TIMELESS LOVE (NATURAL SELF) | TIME-BOUND LOVE (EGO-SELF) |
|---|---|
| Inexhaustible<br>*My love is endless.* | Finite<br>*I'll love you if . . .* |
| Eternal, forever<br>*My love always was and always will be.* | Fades over time<br>*What happened to the love we once had?* |
| Unconditional<br>*I accept you as you are.* | Conditional<br>*If you could just change this one thing . . .* |
| Unlimited<br>*Giving and receiving are one.* | Limited<br>*I'll scratch your back, you scratch mine.* |

We know that we are not our thinking or our beliefs. As we become aware that we are spiritual beings having a human experience, we express timeless love.

In contrast to this easy, free-flowing experience of love is the effort and struggle that many of us associate with being in a relationship. Trying to conform to a relationship based on our invented world of romance or the media's idea of love brings with it thoughts of obligation, responsibility, and effort. Inventing a reality based on illusion is unnatural. The ego *invents*; our spiritual nature *is*.

Most of us go through life gaining only glimpses of this true or natural Self. We experience such transcendent moments when we fall in love, at the birth of a child, in moments of ecstasy, and when we are totally absorbed in the moment, free of our personal thought system of beliefs and personality. We all seek this spiritual essence of our being, but we also fear it and retreat from it because it is a threat to our preconceived notions of ourselves and of the world.

I mentioned earlier that initially I only had a glimpse of the world of timeless love. I hadn't yet *experienced* it. Several years after I quit looking outside for love and began to look within, I went through a very profound experience—an epiphany. My second marriage had reached another crossroads, this time a major one. Insidiously, I had become caught up in my habits of personality and moved away from my true Self. I was talking the talk of love and happiness, but not walking the walk. My wife held firm to her commitment to follow the thread of spirituality in her life, but I was caught up in the world of work, success, and material things. Like many people, I had allowed myself to "fall asleep," lulled back into this world of illusionary happiness. But my wife confronted me in a way that woke me up, very painfully and emotionally at the time, yet later I realized that what she did was necessary.

We were in a marital crisis and I was afraid. I was afraid of losing her, but more important, I was afraid to "let go" of control. Fortuitously, Sydney Banks, my mentor and teacher, was giving a lecture on love and wisdom in San Francisco the weekend following our marital crisis. We both flew out there, lost and extremely unhappy. Though I thoroughly enjoyed and was deeply impacted by the seminar with Syd, I was still frightened and sad. After the seminar, we decided to take a couple of weeks off and drive up the West Coast from California to Washington. The next several days will remain with me for the rest of my life—seared into my memory.

Before we drove up the coast, my wife, Michael, and I stayed with our dear friends for a day. The morning we left, I was playing with their two girls, who were three and five at the time. To this day I don't know what happened while playing with them, but I suddenly felt this incredible feeling of love. I looked at those sweet girls and their innocence, and everything painful seemed to melt away. I felt a deep sense of joy, gratitude, and an indescribable spiritual energy.

As Michael and I began our drive up the coast, I couldn't stop crying. I felt such love for everything, such overwhelming joy that I couldn't contain it. I had to stop the car every few moments just to take in the beauty around me, in me, and in my wife. It didn't matter if we stayed together, it didn't matter if I lived or died, nothing mattered. I felt complete. I felt healed from within. My whole body and mind seemed to be going through a transformation.

For the next four days, I can only describe what I experienced as pure ecstasy. I experienced unconditional love, true love. Those four days had no time. It could have been a moment or several years. It didn't contain an experience of time. It was my first experience with timeless love. No other person could give me that experience; it had to come from within.

Although my experience was profound and complete within itself, it was the beginning of a very significant transformation of my life and our marriage. This insight began to unfold in my everyday life in wonderful ways, but at times I would find myself acting out of old habits and my belief system. This experience had awakened my knowing of what was real and possible, so I didn't mind that I still had one foot in my old habits and one foot in this new world. I could see that as I lived from this new awareness that the old illusionary world of the ego, with its belief system, would automatically wash away.

Not everyone will have the type of prolonged, transcendent experience I just described. Timeless love can reveal itself in many different ways, and no one experience is more valuable or valid than another. One of my students recently shared this story (in her own words) about how timeless love revealed itself in her marriage.

## Love Is a State of Mind, Not an Action

ಲ

I have always loved my husband, and over the years we have had what most would consider an above-average marriage. However, over time the feelings of love began to fade and were replaced with our habits of relating to each other. We would often argue about the kids, money, and trivial things. Nothing major, just everyday normal bickering.

As I began to live more in the moment from the spiritual core of my being, things between Jon and me gradually changed. When he said something I didn't agree with, I would listen deeply to him with openness instead of fighting for my point of view. I would see his total innocence and fall in love with him all over again. [The concepts of "deep listening" and "seeing innocence" are explained in detail in Chapters 4 and 5, respectively.] The deep feelings of love returned to me, and he too began to change. He was more present with me and the kids and started to show his caring more overtly, in little acts of kindness. His true essence began to shine through—the part of him I fell in love with in the first place. That part had never really left; I just stopped seeing it. Instead, I had focused on what he was "doing wrong"; in other words, what he was not doing my way.

Nothing big really changed between Jon and me, but the feeling of love is so strong that some days I feel as though I might burst with joy. I feel this love equally with my children and the many people I encounter each day. I have come to know that love is a state of mind—not an action.

Timeless love is constant. It is not dependent upon whether someone is acting in a way that pleases us. It doesn't diminish over time, but strengthens and deepens.

We may occasionally experience timeless love in a passing moment, but soon we forget it and do not recognize it for its profound importance. It may be present in a glance at our partner, where our eyes meet and we see his or her beauty and feel a surge of love. However, it is just a passing flash of truth, because as we move on to our busy and distracted lives, we push aside the quality and effect of that deep feeling and replace it with our habitual beliefs and emotions. As we grow wiser and more peaceful, however, the fullness of timeless love is revealed to us. We begin to know that love is an undercurrent that is always there, it is the source of all things including us. We feel its power and influence, though we cannot see it with our eyes. We begin to cherish and savor those passing glimpses of truth and beauty, and thus they become more lasting. They shift from the background to the foreground.

As you read these ideas about the nature of timeless love, you may think that it is unattainable. You may be wondering what this kind of deep spiritual love has to do with finding intimacy in your own life. However, if you can first open yourself to an understanding of the nature of timeless love and then consider the possibility that everyone, even you, is capable of realizing it, you will be on your way to experiencing this love yourself. You must have hope and faith to begin this journey, but above all, *willingness* is the first prerequisite. It is a journey worth taking, because timeless love will give you many gifts.

With timeless love:

- You will love unconditionally.
- Your experience of love will continue to grow.
- Insecurity and fear will drop from all your relationships.
- You will be present in your relationships—you will listen deeply, talk from the heart, and appreciate the moment.
- You will be able to forgive.
- You will see conflict as an opportunity for personal transformation.
- Your love will last.
- You will find your own true love within.

I have discovered eight guidelines (although that is an arbitrary number, at the root of each guideline is the same timeless truth) that have helped me and many others realize timeless love in our relationships and within ourselves. I didn't learn them in a book, though many books have spoken of them. I didn't learn them from my teachers, though they tried to direct me to these guidelines. I found them written in my heart, as they come from the innate knowledge available in everyone—waiting to be discovered by each of us. The experience of my own relationships has been my greatest teacher. I am grateful for what I have learned from those who have blessed me with their gifts of love and friendship. Insights about the nature of love have guided me, leaving clues along the way as I traveled the course of my relationships.

I'd like to share with you the eight guidelines of true love that I will explore in detail throughout the rest of the book. I have already introduced the first guideline in this chapter, but it, like all the others, is meant to be reaffirmed in every moment.

## The Eight Guidelines of Timeless Love

1. You *are* the love that you seek—look within.
2. Love can only be found in the present moment.
3. Listen deeply to yourself and to others.
4. Recognize that we all live in a thought-created separate reality.
5. Be aware of your true feelings and emotions as a guidance system.
6. Learn to speak from the heart rather than the intellect.

7. Understand how to let go of the past, through the art of forgiveness.
8. Transform conflict into wholehearted resolution.

As you read about these eight guidelines and the stories of couples who have realized the importance of them in their relationships, open yourself to the possibility that you, too, can have a love that lasts, extends, expands, and grows.

In the next chapter, I will talk about the first guideline, "You *are* the love you seek—look within." Before you can experience love, you have to know where it comes from.

# 2

# LOVE IS WITHIN

THE WIZARD OF OZ was my favorite movie as a child, yet I didn't realize until later in life why I was so drawn to it. The film of Dorothy and her three companions tells the story of what we all have in common—our search for what we think we need to be happy and complete. For Dorothy, it was to return home. For the Tin Woodsman, it was a heart. For the Cowardly Lion, it was courage. And for the Scarecrow, it was a brain. After lots of battles with witches and flying monkeys, these four friends ultimately discovered that a heart, courage, and intelligence were already within them and that home was just a click of the heels away. The Wizard couldn't give them anything they sought; they had to find it for themselves.

So it is with us. We search in so many ways outside ourselves for happiness and love—in possessions, in fame, in power, in addictions, in success and achievements, and most often, in relationships. One of the prize myths of our culture is that if only we could find the "right person" we would be happy. Of course, it sounds like the truth. After all, most of us have been told that the job of our mate is to make us happy, and our job is to make him or her happy. I remember hearing this as a child, but I found out much later in life that it is not the truth.

The truth is quite different. As long as we search outside of ourselves for what can only be found within, we are doomed to disappointment, fear, and despair. When we search for happiness from another person because we believe it is lacking in ourselves, we immediately put tension into that relationship. This pressure, spoken or unspoken, communicates the message, "If you behave just the right way, I'll be happy. If you don't, I'll be unhappy, and it'll be all your fault." This message sets up defensiveness in the other person, because we all intuitively know that we can't really make anyone else feel loved or happy, and we resist trying to do so. On the other hand, we may have the arrogance to think we *can* make someone else happy. "If I love him enough, he will finally be happy." If we believe in this illusion, we are usually disappointed that our beloved isn't grateful for our efforts. In fact, we may discover that he or she feels obligated in some way and resents us for it.

What if we decided to give up this myth of making one another happy and feel loved? What if we realized that love and happiness are already present within us? Think of it for a moment. Love is like the jewel on the bottom of the pond, obscured by the murky water. All of our flailing about clouds the water more and more as we search for the jewel. When we let go, have faith in our innate health, and become still, the silt settles and the clarity of the water emerges in our consciousness. We see the jewel of love that has been there all along.

Most of us, myself included, have spent much of our lives thrashing around in the water, looking for the right person, the perfect job, the best house, or whatever we believe will make us happy. However, if we truly let go of our belief that one magical person must be out there (like Dorothy's wizard) who can make us feel loved and happy, we will discover what we already possess.

# The Jewel at the Bottom

The jewel at the bottom of the pond is ourselves. It is the true or natural Self. It is not separate from all other selves, but united with them all. Like islands that appear separate on the surface, we too think we are separate from everyone else in the world, especially when we long for a relationship or feel alienated from the person with whom we are in a relationship. However, as we go deeper into the human psyche, we see that, like these islands, we extend to the bottom of the sea, where we all stem from the same source, from one ground of being that is our spiritual essence. We are already living in unity; we are only unaware of it.

Contained in this spiritual ground of being is the infinite capacity of all human beings—for true love, creativity, genius, compassion, and self-esteem. From this core of *who we are*, we generate resiliency, the human potential, the indomitable human spirit. Our spiritual essence is what unites us all. When we find the jewel at the bottom of the pond, we have found our innate health and our true love, all in one glittering treasure.

## *Discovery, Knowing, and Acceptance*

Innate health is invisible. We cannot see it with our eyes, but we can readily observe its effects—joy, kindness, forgiveness, strength, hope, and many more virtues that are positive. *Knowing* that it exists within us allows the silt of our thoughts to settle. Then we behold the jewel.

Knowing that the true Self is within is the first step to finding it. The true Self—fully complete, all knowing, all loving, and fulfilled, needs only one thing—*our acceptance*. Nonacceptance of the gift of the true Self and all it contains is what leads to all our searching, desiring, and needing. When we realize who we really are, we remove all the need for excessive thinking—our worry, longing, wanting, and desiring. These are all symptoms of someone who has not yet discovered and accepted his or her natural Self—the jewel.

What is this jewel? It is the spiritual source of our being. It has been called many names—the "God within," the "Atman," the "Self," our "Christ Consciousness," the "Force," our "Higher Self," the "I am," and "Love." Whatever it is called, it does exist, but each of us must discover it for ourselves.

How do we discover this jewel that is our innate health, that is the Self, if it is invisible? The ways to this Self-discovery are infinite. Some find it in religion, others through the experience of a gift of talent, such as art, music, or athletics. Still, others discover the Self through tragedy or near-death experiences. Whatever the catalyst, the revelation of the Self comes to us as an insight, an awareness that is a *feeling*, not an intellectual concept. It is a change in our level of consciousness. Some experience this feeling as a deep sense of peace; others experience it as bliss, love, or oneness with all things. It feels more wonderful than any emotion, yet it feels strangely familiar, like coming home after a long journey. This discovery creates a shift in our level of understanding about the nature of our lives and who we are.

When we realize this inner source of all happiness, this jewel beyond riches, we simultaneously discover true love. Love is within, and knowing that fact frees us up to stop searching for it in another. Paradoxically, when we stop searching for love in another, we extend unconditional love toward others.

## The Innocence of a Thought-Created World

Until I was thirty-three, I spent much of my life looking for someone or something to make me happy. After a failed marriage and a series of romantic disappointments, I felt depressed, disappointed, and disillusioned. Out of exhaustion, I gave up the search. It was then and only then that I began to look within. That is when my true growth began. I stopped searching outside and started listening to my inner voice, my wisdom, and my spiritual core.

It was about this time that I first heard about and attended a seminar in Miami that taught the principles on which this book is based. It was at this seminar that I solidified and validated the direction in which I was intuitively headed. During a three-day conference, I learned about the power of three principles that create all our experience—Mind, Consciousness, and Thought, which I will elaborate on in Chapter 5.

What I learned that weekend would be the major turning point of my life in two ways: I learned the secret to the puzzle of life, and I fell in love with my wife. It was a true double whammy! What appeared to be a coincidence was linked. When I met Michael, I was immediately attracted to her and soon fell deeply in love.

After I returned home from Miami, my first practical learning experience about the principle of how our thinking creates our experience of reality occurred. My head was spinning with new revelations about the mind and how my whole approach to working with my psychotherapy clients would change dramatically. I was also experiencing a flood of emotions about my new love. My love for her grew each day, but my insecure thoughts got the best of me. Was this for real, or was I just following another false lead to another disappointing relationship? Was this true love, infatuation, or lust? Was she feeling the same way, or was it a one-sided romance?

Because I let my insecure thinking take over, I didn't call her for two weeks. Every time I would go to pick up the phone, my fearful thoughts won out and I lost the courage to make the call. Then, one night while I was painting my new kitchen, I had an unexpected flash of insight. My fears and worries were all just insecure thinking, like I had learned about at the conference! With that realization, I picked up the phone and called her. To my delight and amazement, she was feeling exactly the same as I was. Her love for me was growing each day, too. If I hadn't learned about the power of thought to create that experience of insecurity, I might never have picked up that phone. I would never have experienced the past twenty-two years of deep love with my wife.

In listening to my inner wisdom that night, I realized that *I* was making it all up. Innocently, unknowingly, I was using the power of thought to make up my experience. I was soon to realize how innocent we all are when we are convinced that our insecurities are real and that our beliefs are the truth. I'd been having insecure thoughts about my new relationship and had made those thoughts "real." Nevertheless, they were just thoughts. It was like the moment when Toto pulled back the curtain and exposed the fake wizard from Kansas to Dorothy. The jig was up. We are innocent because we are unaware that our ego-belief system is faulty and we act on this illusionary thinking, as I had been doing that night. Fortunately, I realized that the source of *all* my experience—my joys, my hurts, my anger, and my love—was me. I, and I alone, was the creator of my experience. That was the moment when I discovered my true freedom.

When we discover the true source of our experience, it is like looking in the mirror and seeing our life for the first time. We create it all. No matter how much someone loves us or hates us, we are interpreting, perceiving, and creating that experience with our God-given power to think. Isn't that wonderful? We have no one to blame, we are still responsible for our actions, and yet we did what we did in all innocence. We just didn't know any better. But until we see that we're making it up, that we're the creator of our experience, we see our thoughts as an absolute reality "out there."

When we discover that the power of thought creates our experience of life, we open ourselves up to our latent innate health. When we quit stirring up the water and obscuring our view, our innate health is revealed. This calm knowing that allows us to see clearly is called *wis-dom*. Wisdom is seeing life with pure thought without the filter of our habitual thinking—the learned patterns of thought and beliefs that we act on without conscious awareness. Habitual thinking is usually invisible to us. For instance, "I'm always attracted to someone who's not interested in me," "Relationships are difficult," "I worry about my husband because I love him," and "No pain, no gain" are examples of common beliefs and habits of thinking.

The following diagram illustrates what I saw that night in the kitchen, when I was caught up in my insecure, habitual thinking. We look at the other person through a perceptual filter that's clouded with our own past beliefs and judgments, like looking through a glass of dirty water.

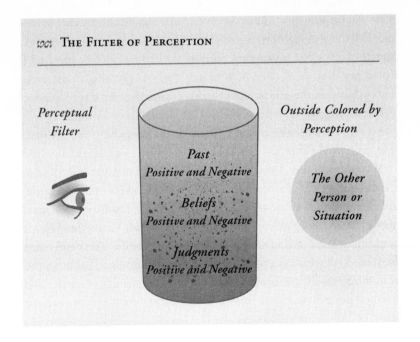

ﱟ **The Filter of Perception**

*Perceptual Filter*

*Outside Colored by Perception*

*Past*
*Positive and Negative*

*Beliefs*
*Positive and Negative*

*Judgments*
*Positive and Negative*

*The Other Person or Situation*

# Observation—The "Natural" Way

Most of us go through life caught in the filter of perception that consists of our habits of thinking: beliefs, attitudes, opinions, past memories, and judgments based on these habitual thoughts. When we see life through this perceptual filter, we "impose" our projections onto life, rather than truly seeing life and each other as they are in reality.

When we are seeing life through our belief system, we are "making meaning" of everything from that personal bias, rather than seeing life objectively. We create an illusion. For example, when I was falling in love with Michael and caught up in my insecure thinking, I was making meaning out of the fact that she hadn't called me:

"She must not like me. If she did, she would have called me by now. She probably has already met someone else. It never works out for me when I meet someone I like this much, why should this be any different?" All these thoughts were just projections of my fears onto the blank screen of life's circumstances. She simply had not called, nor had I called her. But the feeling of timeless love was growing in me each day—that was the truth, my projected thoughts were the illusion. When I recognized that I was thinking this all into existence, I was free—free from the constraints of insecure thinking, free from my past, free from my habits.

With my newfound awareness, I was beginning to experience the difference between a busy, agitated mind that tried to figure out the future, and the powerful awareness of timeless love that results in an experience of peace, insight, and discernment. This wasn't something that I could have tried to do from my old approach to life. The conference presented me with a deeper way of seeing life, and I was beginning to recognize that the truth was within me. I was starting to wake up and become more conscious of how to discern the difference between the truth of my divine nature and the illusion of my ego-belief system. I will go into more depth about this throughout the book.

When I recognized my act of creation—that I was thinking all my insecurities into experience—I changed. I moved from the world of projection to the world of *observation*. It is seeing what is rather than our perception of what is. Observation is seeing life without the filter of personal/habitual thinking. Seeing life from observation calms us down and allows us to follow our heart. When I called Michael, I trusted the timeless love that was within me. I didn't know the future, nor did I think I had to know. I just knew to follow this uncontaminated feeling of pure love. I no longer had any attachment to the outcome. I knew to trust the love.

Thank God I followed my heart that day. In contrast to projection, look at the next diagram to illustrate the power of seeing life through the lens of observation. Imagine the same glass of water, but this time all the water and silt of personal thought are not shaken up and obscuring the view.

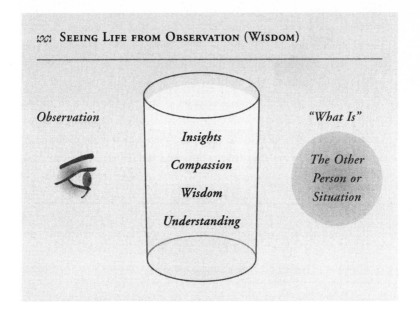

### ∞ Seeing Life from Observation (Wisdom)

*Observation*

*Insights*

*Compassion*

*Wisdom*

*Understanding*

*"What Is"*

*The Other Person or Situation*

### Breaking Free of the Past

ꙮ

Another example will help illustrate this process. Ted and Harriet met in their early forties. He had been divorced and she had never been married. Many issues from his previous marriages existed, including alimony, child support, visitation, and parenting. In short, it appeared, like so many post-divorce relationships, to be very complicated and messy.

As time went on they fell more deeply in love, but they were both filled with fear about commitment, she because she had never been married and he, because he had "failed." They avoided the topic of marriage even though it was in their hearts and on their minds. All her friends warned her to avoid the messy entanglements of blended families and other projected fears. Still, Harriet's love grew.

Ted was torn inside. "How do I dare bring the burden of my past with me into another relationship? How would it work out for Harriet and my kids—she's never been a parent? Will my children let her in? But I love her so much. She is who I want to spend my life with." He avoided the subject as much as possible, but their feelings of love continued to deepen and with it, his thoughts of anxiety and confusion.

I recommended to Ted and Harriet that they listen to my *Slowing Down to the Speed of Love* audiotape set. They intently listened to the tapes, hoping for a solution to their dilemma. As they continued to listen to the principles, they felt less fear, and their true feelings of the heart became crystal clear—they were in love and wanted to commit to each other in marriage. Ted commented, "We realized that our pasts were not what truly mattered. What was in our hearts was where we wanted to put our attention."

They are living in marital bliss and so grateful they listened to their hearts instead of projecting their beliefs and insecure thinking onto the circumstances and each other.

The following table summarizes the difference between uncontaminated *observation*, which occurs in our natural Self, and the habit of *projection* of illusory beliefs onto a situation or another person, which occurs in the false ego-self.

| OBSERVATION | PROJECTION |
| --- | --- |
| Natural or true Self | Ego-self |
| Observes "what is" | Interprets from belief system |
| In the moment | In the past or future |
| Sees differences as interesting | Compares and judges |
| Insights from spiritual intelligence | Memories from belief system |
| Wisdom | Opinions, reactions |

# The Implications of Timeless Love for Relationships

No one can make you feel loved in the truest meaning of the word. Timeless love is the source of who we are, and experiencing a loving feeling is part of that package. Indeed, love is our birthright. Just look at any healthy baby, and you will see that we are born loving, content, serene, and joyful. Once infants' basic needs for food, sleep, and clean diapers are met, they are generally quite content. When they are out of balance, they express it freely and directly.

As long as we believe that someone out there is going to make us feel loved, we will create a false dependency on others that can only lead to conflict, defensiveness, neediness, disappointment, and the ultimate failure of a relationship.

When we discover and uncover that source of true love within our own being, we find that *we* are the love we are looking for. It is only when we discover this love inside that we can love others unconditionally. Until that discovery occurs, we will find ourselves trying to get others to act, feel, and think a particular way. We will use whatever methods we can to change them into what we think we need in order to be happy.

Without this foundation of love within, all of our relationships will end up with us blaming them for disappointing us. It will appear that they misled us or were insincere or used us. It will definitely look like it is someone else's fault that we are hurt, angry, and disappointed.

### Putting Love into a Marriage, Instead of Taking It Out

ΧΣΧ

Kris was an average woman, living an average life. She had an average marriage with an average family of two girls. She and Mike had their ups and downs, but that was normal, she thought, wasn't it? Then Kris started learning the principles of Health Realization, and she began to have an extraordinary life. Her parenting, which had been a difficult struggle, was now a joyous blessing. Her work, which had been tedious and boring, was now full of satisfaction and adventure. Her friendships deepened in love, and she walked through life as though in a dream—except, that is, in her relationship with Mike.

With Mike she felt on edge. She lived in a constant state of fearful anticipation of his angry outbursts, which he directed at her and the girls. They also felt hurt and fearful much of the time in his presence. Kris begged Mike endlessly to go to therapy, to learn the principles that had helped her so much, but he refused. Once, after a particularly big blow-up with one of the girls, she pleaded with him once more. "Won't you please go with me and get help? I'm afraid that if you don't we may not stay together."

She had spoken the unmentionable option: divorce. She couldn't believe she said it, but she felt a newfound sense of resolve, as she grew more content in the rest of her life. Still Mike remained resistant and defiant to the idea of getting help and refused for the hundredth time.

Kris plodded along with her personal changes and found she was moving farther and farther from Mike emotionally. She didn't even know if she loved him anymore. Perhaps it had gone too far and too long, she worried. She was also concerned about the lasting effect of Mike's anger on their daughters.

She asked Mike to go away with her for the weekend, but not unless they had quality time together. She needed to talk to him, heart to heart. On the first night they had dinner at a nice restaurant and had a pleasant time. She could see that he was trying to be loving. Then, at the end of the meal she suggested they wait to get the check before they moved to another part of the restaurant. In her mind, this was a small, insignificant request. Mike, however, exploded with, "Why do you want to start an argument after such a special meal?"

She was baffled and retorted, "I simply wanted to express myself, Mike!" (This type of statement was quite uncharacteristic for her.)

They proceeded to have a heart-to-heart about how she had always avoided conflict because she feared his anger, which had led to her not being herself in the marriage. But she could no longer sacrifice who she was for the sake of keeping the peace; she *would not* do it any longer.

Mike was shocked at her new assertiveness and honesty. "I think I liked the old Kris better," he remarked half kidding.

"Yeah, I bet you do, you always got your way," she said in a lighthearted manner.

Surprisingly, later Mike was actually attracted to Kris being her true Self and accepted her new changes. They ended up having a perfect weekend together and felt very romantic for the first time in a long time.

This, however, is not the end of the story. (As Kris put it, "I am a slow learner.") Time went on and she continued to have doubts about her love for Mike. This was in spite of the fact that Mike was changing a great deal. He didn't blow up anymore. He was thoughtful and kind to her and the kids. However, something was missing. "Have I waited too long to try and work things out?" she often wondered. Had the embers of her love simply burned themselves out?

Then one day, she got an angry and hurt letter from Mike. In it he expressed how miserable he was, how unloved and unappreciated he felt. He hated his life and felt very depressed. Initially she felt defensive and retaliatory, but she stayed calm and didn't respond. She also saw that this letter was a breakthrough for Mike; for once he had truly spoken from the heart. At that moment she saw him as a human being who was unhappy and hurt, by her. She felt deep compassion for him and saw him as a human being, no longer a monster. Later that weekend they had a heart-to-heart and another breakthrough occurred. She finally saw that Mike had truly changed. He was also very open to getting help.

They went back to therapy after that breakthrough conversation and after a couple of sessions her counselor said, "Do you love Mike unconditionally?" She got very defensive and angry. "Of course I do! I love everyone unconditionally."

"Do you love him like you love your daughters, whom you do love unconditionally? Be honest."

The counselor's question burned right through her. She knew the therapist was right, but it took her two weeks of churning before she could admit it. Finally, she realized as she observed herself with Mike and with her daughters that indeed there was a strong difference. With Mike she withheld love until she saw how he was behaving. With her daughters, she just felt love, no matter what they were doing. It was stunning to her. "I don't love Mike unconditionally!"

Gradually, she began to let go of the fear and see Mike for who he now was, rather than the way she had viewed him in the past. She saw a kind and loving person. She fell in love with him again. One night she was staring at him, full of love. He noticed and asked, "What are you looking at?" She responded, "I see a soft and loving man."

"Yeah," he joked, "the new and improved Mike."

From that moment on she saw Mike not through the lens of fear and projection, but as his true Self. She felt unconditional love for him, once she realized that timeless love was what she could put into the marriage, without expectation of what she got out of it. Mike too has changed. In the light of unconditional love, he has grown more kind, more loving, more himself.

Kris realized that she had not been responding to Mike from her true Self. Our true Self naturally extends unconditional, timeless love to our partner. Kris's new awareness did not make her blind to Mike's insecurities or low moods, but it did give her new vision that enabled her to see beyond his behavior to his spiritual core. She was then able to clearly see solutions to their problems. When Mike experienced love from her that was unconditional he felt free from judgment, which allowed him room to change. Most of us respond positively in the presence of love. Timeless love is to our partner like a greenhouse is to plants; it is the perfect environment for the awareness of one's natural Self to bloom.

Kris and Mike are like two people who just met and are seeing each other fresh each day, with all the excitement and love they ever dreamed of.

In the next chapter we will explore the second guideline to timeless love—"Love can only be found in the present moment." Living in a state of presence is the key to experiencing intimacy in any relationship.

# 3

# LIVING IN A STATE
# OF PRESENCE

BEING PRESENT IS an access point to timeless love. When we are fully
aware and living from our spiritual consciousness, we perceive the true
essence of others. When the channel between two people is unclut-
tered with distraction, judgment, past memories, or worry about the
future, they enter the precious present and truly feel connected.

Presence is a state of mind that is calm, quiet, and not caught up in
habitual thought. In any relationship, how often one is present determines the quality of the connection between two or more people.
When people are preoccupied, they focus on their personal thoughts
of the past, the future, or judgment of the present through their individual thoughts and beliefs. The state of mind of nonpresence can be
focused on a variety of thoughts—evaluation, distraction, analysis,
comparison, and agreement/disagreement—but they are all forms of
*projection* of habitual thinking. In contrast to the clear view of life that

we see when we live as our true Self and observe life without judgment, projection "filters" reality through the lens of our ego beliefs and thoughts.

How do we experience presence? How do we move away from habitual thinking and projection so that we can experience the present moment and the intimacy that comes with it? Presence is not something we do; it is who we are. It has nothing to do with time, as we think of it—being present is timeless. When we are being our true or natural Self, we are present. In the world of the true Self, all that exists is the eternal present moment, where our thinking is wise, creative, new, and outside of our personal frame of reference.

As you read this book, you may find yourself slipping in and out of being present. One moment you are so captured by the words that you forget you are reading a book, you forget where you are, your surroundings disappear, and you are absorbed by the content and the feeling. The next moment you are distracted by someone or something in the environment, by your body, or by the activation of your memories. When this happens you might have to go back over what you just read because you weren't present while you were reading. You may have read the words, but your mind was focused elsewhere. If you aren't present, you can't experience what *is*, you experience only what you *think*.

Let me give you a personal example to illustrate the meaning of presence in a relationship. I recall being on my honeymoon with Michael on a canoe trip in the northern Minnesota wilderness. We had been paddling much of the day and were close to our destination campsite. I was eager to get to the campsite, set up camp, and enjoy the rest of the day. I was paddling hard, and I noticed that Michael had quit. Irritated, I asked her what she was doing.

"Look at those rocks, Joe, they're incredible!" she replied, seeming to ignore my question.

"What rocks?" I responded in a puzzled manner.

"Don't you see the colors? The reds, the pinks, the lichen, the greens and yellows."

To me, the rocks looked gray. All I saw was the blur of the rocks as I rushed to get to camp. But I was just so struck by how awed she was that I took a second look. I put down my paddle, came into that moment, and looked. I was amazed at all the color that unfolded before me as I quieted my mind and actually looked at the rock wall. A wall of rocks formed a channel at that point in the lake. The late afternoon sun hit the walls and created a vivid, multihued reflection in the water, which blew me away.

That incident was very significant for me in many ways. I realized that my wife lived in a world different from mine. She was usually in the moment and perceived the natural beauty around her. I, on the other hand, had been living my life always trying to go faster, always anticipating the next moment and rarely living in this one. After that incident, I wondered how much I had missed in life and began to appreciate her view of the world and who she is as a person. That day, a whole new way of looking at life revealed itself to me. As the trip continued she would point out the beauty of the clouds, the water patterns, or the grain of wood in a tree. It was as if I were seeing things for the first time, even though I had been around them all my life.

## Living in the Moment Within Relationships

When we are present, we perceive a different reality—one that is filled with beauty, awe, and inspiration. Nothing in the external reality changes, only our awareness of it. The same is true for our relationships, which is why living in the moment is one of the secrets of true love. When we live in the moment and are with someone we love, we see beyond our concepts of who that person is, concepts that are based on our past experiences with him or her. We see past our expectations, our disappointments, and the distractions of our other thoughts. By being present we are able to see beyond our mate's behavior, even if he or she is out of balance and in a negative state, to the essence of who that person is. We see through to the innate beauty and perfection of the other—the part we fell in love with in the first place. By being in the present, we not only protect ourselves from having a reaction to our mate's behavior, but we also gain the added benefit of not throwing fuel on a potentially explosive situation. Being present helps us see the innocence of others: that they are stuck in the faulty belief system of the ego. (See Chapter 2 and Chapter 8 for more on the concept of innocence.) It also helps us to see how to respond to the other from our deeper intelligence, rather than react to him or her from our insecure habits.

When we are in a state of presence we are being our natural Self, which is pure love—understanding, compassionate, nonjudgmental, forgiving, and accepting. Being present and aware of the true Self is magical. It takes us to an undiscovered world, one we have not yet experienced in our relationship or in life. It is never boring, dull, or uninteresting. It is full of life—adventure, awe, inspiration, and delight. As we experience the natural Self more often, we drop into this experience of presence more easily. We desire to live nowhere else, because we realize that this is what we have always really been looking for in our search for fulfillment and happiness. How do we recapture our natural Self?

I remember that I first experienced the joy of presence as an adult when I was exposed to the principles of Health Realization that this book is based on. I had become a very serious professional psychologist. I was always analyzing myself and everyone around me. I had become totally absorbed in my ego-self.

I arrived in Miami anticipating a typical psychology conference— reading professional papers, intellectual discussions on the dynamics of mental illness, family issues, and other "dry" subjects. To my discomfort and surprise, the participants of the conference were very joyful, fun-loving, and happy. I felt left out, like the new kid on the block. I also felt very suspicious.

However, before long I found myself "caught up" in the moment with the other participants and I began having fun. I felt like a child again. I hadn't felt this way in a long time. I don't remember the particulars of what we did that weekend, but it was all done spontaneously and in a spirit of playfulness. I felt like myself again. In hindsight, I was swept up in the experience of presence without really knowing how it happened, but I liked it. I wanted to learn how to live in that feeling more of the time. Although I was skeptical that an adult could feel this way and still be responsible, I was *willing* to consider that it was

---

∞ To LIVE IN A STATE OF PRESENCE, YOU NEED TO DO THE FOLLOWING:

---

- Be willing.
- Realize that now is all that truly exists.
- Don't project your habitual thinking.
- Accept that presence is not something you do; it is something you are.
- Listen deeply.
- Understand that presence is just being yourself.

possible. That is all you really need to do to live with more presence in your life: consider the possibility that you can.

## The Natural Self and the Ego-Self

Do you ever wonder, "How does life work? Who am I, really? Am I my personality? Am I the sum total of all the good and bad traits I've accumulated since birth? Or am I something more?"

Some of us think that we can change our personalities to eliminate the traits we don't like and acquire the ones we desire. Others think they are trapped by their past and circumstances and that they must accept their fate. I have great news! You don't have to change your personality to recapture your true Self. As a matter of fact, all the effort at self-improvement and self-analysis actually further separates us from the true or natural Self. Working on yourself to be your Self is like trying to find that jewel at the bottom of the water by flailing in the water—it only obscures the jewel from sight.

As young children, we operated initially more from the natural Self—we were curious, open, and unprejudiced about the world. The true or natural Self experiences the world as interesting, fun, and beautiful. We feel natural self-esteem, unconditional love, compassion, and abundant joy. Life is carefree—we are in touch with our true feelings, express them easily, and move on. The natural Self is also full of insights, wisdom, and common sense. Therefore, it gives us very practical tools to help us live our lives—it gives us solutions to problems when we need them, it is the source of creative thinking, and it allows us to live in the world of relationships with greater understanding and ease.

This natural Self is who we really are, but we've lost awareness of our true identity. Our true Self easily expresses timeless love because we *are* love. In this state, we easily see solutions because we see beyond the lower level of awareness that created the problem in the first place.

When unaware of our spiritual nature, we search outside ourselves for love and happiness.

As we grow older, we become more conditioned by our environment—we are innocently taught many habits and beliefs by our parents, teachers, and friends, and we accept many misconceptions of society as well. From this, we create a personal belief system. The more we learn, the more we begin to mistrust the natural Self, to judge ourselves as being "different," "unacceptable," or "not as good as" others. We do this in hundreds of ways—when competing in sports or academics; looking at our physical appearance; creating definitions of beauty; or establishing our likes, dislikes, and personal interests. We do this all in the hope of being loved and accepted, only to find out later that we betrayed the true Self.

I recently saw the popular movie *Billy Elliot*, about a young man who finds his true Self as he grows up in a poor area near London. His dad and family are all working class and value being tough and violent. Billy is interested in ballet, much to his dismay initially. However, as he sneaks into ballet class week after week instead of going to his boxing lessons, he and his teacher discover that he is a gifted dancer. When his dad and brother find out, he is humiliated by them for acting "like a girl" and teased mercilessly. In spite of their negative reaction, he listens to his true Self and follows his passion and joy. Eventually, he becomes an accomplished ballet dancer. His father and brother realize his gift for dance and ultimately, to their credit, they support him wholeheartedly.

Billy Elliot is a fine example of someone who stayed true to his natural Self and resisted the social pressures to conform to his cultural belief system. When we are our true Self, we are present and in the moment. We are capable of following our true feelings, which guide us and show us how to live our dreams.

Through misunderstanding, we soon develop habits, self-concepts, beliefs, opinions, and attitudes. As we learn fear and insecurity our awareness of the natural Self begins to shrink. For many, the natural Self becomes covered almost completely by a highly developed ego-self. As we lose awareness of the natural Self, we inevitably experience ourselves as separate and alone. We experience an inner emptiness that we spend much of the rest of our life trying to fill up. We long for that carefree feeling of early childhood, but see it as "unrealistic." Without awareness of the natural Self, we can't live in the present very much of the time. We are prisoners of our own thoughts.

However, as we begin to "remember" who we are and experience insights from our inner wisdom, we glimpse our true Self. The natural Self is always present; we just haven't recognized it or known how to trust it. The table that follows illustrates the difference between the natural Self (which shares in unity with all of creation), and the ego-self (which thinks it is separate and alone).

| NATURAL SELF | EGO-SELF |
| --- | --- |
| Timeless love | Time-bound love |
| Oneness/Unity | Separateness |
| Insights/Truth | Beliefs/Illusion |
| Effortless way of being | Effortful way of being |
| Source of innate health | Source of suffering |
| Creativity | Beliefs |

Habits are not inherently good or bad. It is how conscious or aware we are as we use them. We all need to learn many things, most of which give us the skills to live our lives: everything from learning to tie our shoes to assimilating a new language, to training to ride a bike or drive a car. However, when we live our lives totally from the ego-self, we lose the power of wisdom and discernment—that is, we are no longer able to differentiate between what is helpful (life-giving and sustaining) and what is harmful (unloving, damaging, life-taking). The ego is a self-validating thought system that perpetuates its own beliefs in an often self-destructive way. Addictions, such as alcoholism, are a classic example of this. Arguing to always be right in a relationship is another. These habits are self-defeating and alienating. They keep us from being ourselves and truly seeing our connection to others. We will speak in more depth about the ego-self later and how we can avoid the traps of our learned habitual thinking while benefiting from the positive aspects of learning and habits. We will talk about the role emotions have as a guidance system to the powers of discernment. For now, it is important to know the difference between the natural Self and the ego-self so that we can understand how to access a state of presence.

## Presence—A Natural Way of Being

Presence is being in a natural way. When we are present, our thinking becomes insightful and it has a different quality that we don't usually associate with its process. We tend to conceive of thinking as an analytical process that is verbal and intellectual. We also think of it as something we do. However, consider this: whenever you are present in the moment, absorbed by a task or a sport or being captured by beauty, you are not conscious that you are thinking. It is almost as if the thoughts are *flowing through you*. This kind of present-moment thinking is effortless and automatic. While in this present-minded state of being, we are observing life rather than projecting our habitual thoughts about life.

When we are in the present moment it is as though the ego-self is moved aside and something else takes over. This something else is the natural Self, as opposed to our belief system and ego. The ego wants control, predictability, and to be right. When we let go and drop into the flow of the moment we lose all that, but gain something that is far greater—we gain love. For love is the essence of the present moment. Love is all that exists when we drop into our most natural state, the state of presence.

Perhaps the best illustration of presence is early childhood. Have you ever observed a young child at play? I love recalling our first Christmas with our granddaughter, who is now three. As we watched her open her gifts, we were struck by how she was just as fascinated with the paper and the box as she was with what was inside the wrapping. She was equally amazed by a large wooden spoon we let her play with as she was by the musical toy with ten gadgets, recorded voices, lights, and numerous noises emanating from it.

Allison is no different from any young child—they are constantly living in the moment and have no concept of what is more valuable or interesting than what engages them at the present moment—*everything* in life is interesting! Young children live their lives in a state of endless curiosity and interest.

We are drawn to young children because we love to be around that feeling of awe, joy, and unconditional love. Just watch a group of very serious employees' faces when someone brings a baby into the room—instant transformation. People drop what they are doing because they're drawn to that innocence and presence.

As we go through life and mature, we accumulate more and more conditioned thoughts and beliefs. This conditioning begins in childhood. This is when children start to say things like, "I didn't get as much as Johnnie!" or "I like this dolly better than that dolly." Unhappiness and disappointment begin. As we become adolescents and adults, we become more sophisticated in our likes and dislikes, in our idea of what it takes to be happy and enjoy ourselves. Thus, we trap ourselves in a world of comparison, disappointment, jealousy, and envy. We want what we don't have. Operating from only the habit-self creates unhappiness.

How do we recapture the presence that was so natural to us as young children? Whenever we return to the present moment, as I did when I slowed down enough to see the rock formations, the same feelings we experienced as young children magically reappear!

## Slowing Down to the Speed of Presence

When we are present with another human being, the clouds of personal belief disappear, and we see the other person as they are in this moment, a pure being unfettered by our preconceived notions of who we think he or she is. We see his or her natural Self. When two people truly fall in love with each other, they are present and experiencing one another from their true nature—love. We often hear people say that "love is blind," because while a person is "in love," he or she sees the other in his or her true state. When the state of the ego returns—the "toxic" habits of beliefs, judgments, and opinions—we bring the clouds of habitual thought back to distort our vision of the other. In fact, we do this same process with all of life. When we view everything from the natural Self, we feel awe, wonder, and joy—we experience timeless love. As soon as our personal belief system kicks in, all the fascination of life disappears.

One of the reasons human beings like to make love is because that is when many of us can completely lose ourselves in the moment and forget all of our personal thoughts—we slow down to the moment. However, if we can't forget the day's worries and problems, making love is less enjoyable and sometimes even impossible to do.

Being present in a relationship means seeing the other person through a clear channel of thought—without the obscurity of the past or the future. When we are present in our relationship, we see through to the heart of the other. It is much like falling in love in the truest sense of the phrase, not just infatuation.

When we fall in love we don't see the externals of the person—looks, personality, or behavior. We see past those particulars to an invisible presence. This "falling-in-love" experience is really the closest most of us come to seeing life in its spiritual form. Unfortunately, we quickly return to our personal thoughts and begin judging, comparing, and expecting the other person to be something other than what he or she is in that essence. When this happens, we say we are "falling out of love" or "seeing the other person more realistically."

Consider thought as the blue sky. If the sky is cloudless, it is clear and unobstructed—we can see through it as if it didn't exist. If a windstorm comes up and creates a cloud of dust, our view is less clear. The more "stormy" our thinking, the more obscurely we see life and those we love. When my mind is busy and filled with distraction or judgments, the same habits my wife has that are endearing in a clear state of mind become irritating and bothersome—due to my unclear state of mind. A clear state of mind is a mind filled with presence.

People often say that as the years go by in a relationship, couples lose the spark they once had; they become bored with one another or, worse yet, they fall out of love. In most cases, this is not a function of time but a lack of presence. I watched my own parents, after sixty years of marriage, fall more in love each year. In my own marriage of twenty years, I know that whenever I am present with Michael, my love grows deeper. I never tire of her because she is never the same person. When I am in the moment, I see her ane v. She is more fascinating to me, more attractive, more enjoyable to be with, with each passing year. This is not the case with many married couples because they live in the past, in an illusory world of conditioned thought. They think they already know their mate. After all, whatever there is to learn about the other person, they certainly would have discovered it by now. How wrong they are.

When we discover the source of timeless love—of presence—we enter into a world of unceasing change and transformation where boredom is impossible. The world of the present moment is infinite, it is eternally changing, and it has endless depth. When we discover what is within us, the natural Self, we discover the source of timeless love—a reflection of that same Self.

## Presence Breaks Us Free of Past Habits and Reawakens Our Love

William James, the founder of American psychology, once said, "Genius is nothing more than seeing life in an unhabitual way." You could say the same about timeless love: it is nothing more than seeing your lover in an unhabitual way. When we drop our habits of seeing each other from a past-based perspective and instead look anew in this moment, love comes back to life. Love returns because as the essence of the natural Self, it has never left us. We have only lost consciousness of its existence for the moment.

I recall an incident that a friend once related to me. One night, he came home from work and sat down in front of his big-screen TV and went into his habitual trance state. It was his way of de-stressing from his workday. His wife began reciting the litany of the day's events with the children and asking when was he going to take out the trash and get to that repair he promised her he would do last week. He tuned her out and began hearing the echo of all the past nights when she had done the same thing. He could feel his tension mounting and a fight brewing. Suddenly, he realized he was caught up in his thinking and came back to the present. He asked her to repeat what she had been saying, and this time he really listened to her. He heard the same words, but this time he heard what was underneath the words—she missed him.

He reached out to her and held her and said, "You miss me, don't you?"

She sank into his arms and they embraced for a long time. He realized that he had been caught up in seeing her through the past and not listening to her at all. No wonder she was angry. He apologized for being so insensitive.

When we are present and something needs to be communicated, we have the state of mind to hear it. This is called listening and talking from the heart.

## Shifting Out of the Fast Lane

I remember another trip up to the northern part of the state to our cabin. My wife and I often go to the cabin, which is a place of great tranquility, quiet, and beauty. In the past, the trip there was dreadfully long for me—five hours that seemed to never end. I couldn't wait to get to the cabin so I could relax and enjoy myself. The trip back was equally dreadful. "Back to reality," I'd think. "If only I could live at the cabin." The time there passed so quickly, yet it was so full and enjoyable while we were there.

One weekend while we were on our way up, I began complaining about how monotonous the trip was and how I couldn't wait to get there. Michael said casually, "We're already on vacation, so why don't you enjoy the journey instead of waiting to get there?" I halfheartedly defended myself, but I knew she was right. I decided to relax and was amazed at how beautiful the scenery on the road suddenly appeared. Because I was in the moment and calm, I saw beauty all around me.

Michael and I had a great talk on the way up, and the time flew by. When we arrived at the cabin, I was already relaxed, and I continued to unwind the whole three days. As I slowed down to the moment even more, I began to feel so close to Michael and so much in love. It was then that I realized that living in the moment was being my true Self—and that intimacy was a natural result of timeless love. Since that time, I certainly can't say I have always been in the moment, but I realize now that whenever I feel disconnected from her, the problem is not with her. The problem is that one or both of us have lost our awareness of the natural Self. When we are in a state of presence, we have slowed ourselves down to the speed of love. In this state of being, we experience timeless love. Have you ever been with someone you loved and felt that time stood still? This is how it feels to be in the moment, to be fully present in your relationship. This is when we enter the "eternal now" that is often spoken of in spiritual litera-

## ∞ PRACTICING PRESENCE

Whenever you are aware that you are not in a state of presence, practice the following guidelines:
- Just be aware, don't judge or analyze why you aren't present.
- Take a moment to be quiet, and breathe.
- Listen deeply.
- Don't do anything and you will automatically return to a state of presence.

ture. In this eternal now, we experience our true nature—compassion, gratitude, love, tenderness, caring, and joy. The veils of personal beliefs are removed, and we open the door to the spiritual reality that is always there but hidden from view by our personal thinking.

# The Benefits of Being in a State of Presence

In summary, presence benefits our relationships in numerous ways:

- We listen better.
- We are aware of our connection and experience more intimacy.
- We see each other anew, in a fresh way that reflects who we are in this moment.
- We break free of our old habits.
- We see the other person's essence instead of our projection or memory of who they are.
- We experience time as elastic and richer.
- We can see when the other person has changed.
- We experience feelings of deep love.

# 4

# LISTEN DEEPLY

IF YOU ONLY have time to read one chapter in this book, this would be the one. Deep listening is the most important skill to develop to have a relationship based on timeless love. Deep listening is never in a hurry, it never judges, it is defenseless, and it accepts the other person as he or she is.

Deep listening encompasses much of what has been said thus far. To listen deeply, you must be in the present moment, your mind must be quiet, and you must be able to recognize when you are thinking in a way that distracts you. In addition, when you listen deeply, you will be living from your core of innate health—your natural Self—where you will be in a state of observation, not in a projection of your thought system.

I used to think I was an above-average listener. After all, I was trained in psychology, I taught other people how to listen, and I was an expert in family and couples therapy.

Then one night many years ago, my own wife told me in a firm but loving way that I was a terrible listener. I was shocked. How could she, an untrained professional, tell me, a marriage counselor, that I was a poor listener? My clients thought I was a great listener. What could she be thinking? However, she was unwavering. She meant what she said.

I'll never forget that night. We were in the aptly named Bad Habit Cafe. I was shocked, horrified, and embarrassed, but after my initial defensiveness, I realized the importance of what she was saying. Somewhere inside, I knew that she was right. In not listening to her I had hurt her deeply and many others around me. I realized that though I could hear her words, I didn't know how to listen to the essence of what she was telling me. I didn't know how to listen wholeheartedly; I only knew how to listen with my intellect.

I didn't learn how to listen that night, but I did realize the most important ingredient I needed to have to do so: I became willing.

The next year felt like a crash course in listening. I realized how much of my listening, no matter how well intended, was an interpretation from my ego-based point of view. I would hear what my wife or anyone else was saying and then run it through my thought system, fitting it into a category or belief that I was already familiar with. I would conclude that I knew what she and others in my life were saying without having a clue of what they were actually trying to communicate.

Since that night in the Bad Habit Cafe, I have become a student of deep listening. Becoming a deep listener is like learning to play a musical instrument. The more you master it, the more you feel like a beginner. Just when you think you are a great listener, you lose humility, which is one of the essential elements to deep listening. So, we are all beginners in the art of listening.

However, like playing an instrument, the rewards of each little step in the process are immeasurable. If you can learn to listen deeply, you will do more for your relationships than you can imagine. Even if you are not currently in a significant relationship, listening deeply will help you with all relationships and with life in general. Communication at the office, with friends, your children, social occasions, and even an ordinary shopping trip can all be satisfying and fulfilling exchanges if you are listening deeply.

**Deep listening allows you to:**
- Hear the *essence* of what someone is communicating with his or her words
- Feel *connected* to the other person and be touched by him or her
- Feel *compassion* for others
- Find *humility*
- *Calm* down and relax
- *Heal* hurts and misunderstandings
- Easily *navigate* through life
- Gain *clarity* and insights
- Be *present* and experience our true Self

## What Is Deep Listening?

Deep listening occurs when your mind is quiet. Your thoughts are flowing rather than crowding your mind with distractions, interpretations, judgments, conclusions, or assumptions. Your mind is open, curious, and interested—as though you were hearing this person for the first time. Deep listening applies not only to communication with another, but also to listening to ourselves and to life in general. The goal of deep listening is to hear beyond the words of the other person and yourself, to the essence of what the words and feelings are pointing to. Your mind and heart are joined in union—you are listening wholeheartedly.

Deep listening becomes effortless as your awareness increases. It is more like listening lightly to your favorite music, the sound of a stream rushing by, or a bird singing. When we listen to these delightful sounds we are under no pressure, we aren't analyzing or figuring out—we are simply letting the feelings and sounds affect us. Deep listening is not defensive, argumentative, or intrusive. It is not about struggling to analyze or interpret. It is a purely receptive state of mind. In a state of deep listening, we realize our oneness. We realize that we are not separate, but truly one spirit—we are connected.

When we listen deeply, we let go of any beliefs we have about the other person. We let go of our prejudices and past memories of him or her.

Here is an example of deep listening in action.

### The Power of Deep Listening

꿈

One day, Julie and Jeff were talking about the possibility of getting together with another couple who lived on the other side of the country. On prior occasions, every time Jeff would make the suggestion, he sensed that Julie had a resistance to it. This time, she opened the subject. She said, "Let's talk about getting together with Bob and Celeste."

"I get the feeling you aren't sure about getting together with them, is that right?" Jeff asked.

"I'm not exactly sure what's going on with me about it. Can you just listen to me for a moment until I get some clarity?"

"Sure." Jeff cleared his mind of his agenda and just listened to her. He opened himself up to seeing a new possibility.

She said, "I want to get together with them, but I just feel like staying home at this point. After the holidays and all the traveling we did this fall, I don't seem to be interested in doing anything but staying home. Perhaps they could come here? Maybe we could tell them we'd like to get together and let them know we'd like them to come here."

"I'm open to that. I'll call them and take it to the next step and see what happens."

As it turned out, other circumstances came up, and their friends couldn't get together with them anyway. If Jeff had tried to pursue his agenda of going out West, it would have been a waste of time. More important, by not pressing his point and by being open to what his wife had to say, Julie felt *heard* and *respected* for her feelings.

In the past, Jeff might have handled this situation differently. He might have had thoughts like, "She never wants to do anything!" He would have tried to logically convince her of why they should go where their friends live: because it was warmer there, because they lived by the ocean, or whatever else supported his agenda. In contrast, deep listening enabled Jeff to understand and respect Julie's feelings, and he felt fine about the outcome of their talk. This nonpressured approach to listening helped Julie sort out her own feelings, which is conducive to gaining insights. And he felt loving, secure, and quiet while he was deeply listening to Julie.

This interaction led to closeness and connection between Jeff and Julie. It helped him to see the situation in a new way and to let go of his agenda, and it helped her get clarity on what she wanted to do.

The goal of deep listening is to be touched by the other person and to hear the essence of what he or she is saying. Deep listening is based on unconditional love and respect. It stems from the natural Self and from timeless love. In addition, it slows you down to the speed of love.

The opposite of this type of listening is what I will call "effortful listening."

## Effortful Listening

Like deep listening, effortful listening has the purpose of trying to understand the other person. Unfortunately, it doesn't accomplish its goal. However, the greatest difference between effortful listening and deep listening is that instead of being based on love, effortful listening is based on *fear*. Most of us, including me, were raised by example to listen defensively and with a lot of thinking going on in our heads—feeling judged and rehearsing our rebuttal. No matter how well intended our listening is, if we are having insecure thoughts or are fearful in any way, we are operating from our ego-self and thus, our listening will become effortful. We will achieve the opposite of what we intended, for effortful listening blocks the flow of understanding and feeling of connection between people.

Effortful listening takes us into our intellectual thinking. As soon as the intellect takes over, we begin processing the content of what the other is saying. We analyze it to make meaning based on something that is already in our thought system, such as an association, concept, assumption, or belief. Alternatively, we evaluate it to see if we agree or disagree with what the other person is saying; we engage in judgment or blame. We are engaged in a projection of our personal habitual thinking instead of observing the other person without expectations, assumptions, or analysis. All of these ways of using the gift of thought keep us stuck in our personal reality and belief system and prevent deep listening.

Effortful listening is like trying to grasp at water with our hands. Only an open, cupped hand can hold water. Trying to grasp what someone else is trying to communicate with his words and gestures always takes us back to our past memories. In so doing, we create a middleman between the essence of what the other person is trying to communicate and our understanding of it. That middleman is like a filter that blocks the true meaning and combines what remains on the surface with our analysis, evaluation, and judgment.

A student recently told me a story that illustrates the transition from effortful listening to deep listening. Here is that story in her own words.

### Deep Listening and Boundaries

∞

I was really enjoying my morning; I was taking my time to do all the things I had to do that day. Then my husband, Bill, called and said that I needed to help a friend of his who was in a real bind. Bill was supposed to help him out, but something came up at his office and he just couldn't. He assumed I was at home with little to do and that surely I would just comply, like I normally do. Initially, I said "yes," but as I listened inside to my common sense I realized that I resented his assumption that I would help when I already had my morning planned. Instead of getting angry with him, I just calmly told him that I couldn't do it. I let him know that ordinarily my habit might be to just jump in and help, but I was learning to respect my time and myself more. He got really put off by my new attitude. I didn't react; I just listened deeply. He sensed my self-assurance and responded, "Well, maybe there is another way. In fact, I do know who could help him out. Thanks, anyway." The whole situation would have normally been an opportunity for resentment and martyrdom on my part and anger on his part. Instead, by listening deeply to myself and to him, the situation resolved itself.

As you can see in this example, it is important to listen to ourselves deeply, as well as to others. I will talk more about listening to ourselves in Chapter 6.

## Distracted Listening

Distracted listening is another way that we avoid listening deeply. In our fast-paced world, this is perhaps the most common form of listening, which is no listening at all. Distracted listening is like having two radio stations on at the same time—we can't hear either clearly and there is a lot of static. Distracted listening occurs when our mind is busy or when we are multitasking, trying to do two things at once. Have you ever been engaged in a conversation with someone and suddenly realize that you have no idea what she has just been saying? Or, have you ever been driving your car and the radio announcer says he is about to play a particular song, which is one of your favorites? Moments pass, and your mind is somewhere else, and he comes back on the air and says, "We have just heard _____," the song you were waiting for, and you don't remember hearing it. This is a good example of distracted listening.

In our hurried world we are all guilty, myself included, of a great deal of distracted listening. We seem to be more interested in the conversations in our heads than each other. Or, in our attempt to get more done, we try to do more than we can humanly handle. The price we pay is the quality of our relationships and the quality of our lives. It is only when we slow down to the speed of love—of this moment—that we can listen deeply and feel our connection.

## The Signs of Effortful or Distracted Listening

How can we tell when we are engaging in effortful or distracted listening? We will feel tense, "spacey," unfocused, distant, uncomfortable, defensive, urgent, or anxious. The body is like a sensor that tells us when we move out of deep listening and into effortful or distracted listening. It speaks to us through sensations and emotions of comfort and discomfort. These are all welcomed signals that let us know we have moved out of deep listening and into a form of listening that will not lead to transformation and healing. In fact, effortful listening usually ends up becoming an argument, debate, or quagmire of intellectual discussion that leaves both people feeling misunderstood and frustrated.

Unfortunately, this is how most of us have been taught to listen in our culture. We interrupt each other, react, take things personally, jump to false conclusions, and rehearse what we are going to say while the other person is talking. It is no wonder that after many millennia of existence we still have so much violence, war, and conflict among nations, races, communities, families, and couples.

Effortful listening and distraction are exactly the way I listened for much of my life, and I still do so occasionally to this day. Whenever I listen in an effortful way, no understanding occurs, only a solidifying of my point of view and my need to be right. This need belongs to the world of the ego-self, which has no place in timeless love. The negative feelings associated with the ego—tension, control, fear, stress— are all red flags that we have moved out of our natural Self. We must learn to recognize when our ego or intellect has taken control and be willing to drop it and return to deep listening.

In most effortful listening or distracted conversations, two people are hearing their own thoughts rather than listening to what the other person is saying. To illustrate this point, think of listening like a walkie-talkie. With a walkie-talkie, you can listen when the button is up, but not be heard. When you press down the button, you can speak and be heard if the other person's button is up, but you cannot hear the other person. With a walkie-talkie, you are either in "talk mode" or "listen mode"; you cannot listen and talk at the same time. It is the same with true communication. We cannot engage in the inner talk of analyzing, processing, distraction, making meaning, or judging and deeply listen at the same time. When we are engaged in effortful or distracted listening, we have essentially pushed down our walkie-talkie buttons throughout the entire conversation and are therefore hearing only our own thoughts. Thus, we are missing what is truly being said on the other end of the conversation. When we are living as our natural Self, we are living in a state of awareness. We can gain or lose that awareness in a second. We will know by the feeling in that second if we are experiencing the natural Self or the ego-self. Remember: the ego-self knows nothing of timeless love—the natural Self *is* love.

## Listening as a Way of Life

Take a moment to reflect on what we have just discussed. How would you apply this in your life? The next time you are engaged in a conversation, engage in deep listening. Notice when your mind moves into distracting thoughts, judgments, memories, interpretations, interruptions, wanting to say something, trying hard to listen, or anything else that takes you out of the moment and out of deep listening. It is very important that you don't do anything more than notice when you have moved out of deep listening—don't judge yourself or give yourself a lecture, feel guilty, or try to figure out why you weren't listening or for how long—just notice that you aren't listening and let it go. This gentle noticing will take you back to listening in the moment. Over time, you will get better and better at deep listening; you only need to be willing.

# The Four *C*s of Deep Listening

As we become better listeners, we will notice many wonderful benefits for our relationships and ourselves. In fact, all aspects of our lives will benefit from an understanding of this type of listening, not just our intimate relationships. I teach this same understanding to managers, salespeople, police, medical personnel, and therapists.

I will summarize the benefits of deep listening in four areas, which I call the "Four *C*s of Deep Listening." It calms, cares, connects, and communicates.

1. It *calms* down both the listener and the speaker.
2. It leads to feelings of *caring* and *compassion*.
3. It makes us feel *connected*.
4. It greatly helps us *communicate*.

## Calm

Deep listening has the immediate effect of calming you down and bringing you back to your natural Self. As a counselor, I have to be a deep listener to help other people. One of the added benefits of doing therapy, or any other time I deeply listen, is that I notice I feel much more relaxed afterwards, no matter how upset I was beforehand. When we listen deeply, we step outside our own problems and clear our minds of our personal thoughts. We are in the state of presence—this is the true Self. In a sense, deep listening is just like meditation. The goal of meditation is to let go of our thoughts, let them drift away. Deep listening has the same goal.

When I am listening to my loved one, I have to be present and let go of everything that is on my mind. For example, this morning I was on the Internet and answering E-mails. Michael, who had just woken up, came in, and began to tell me about a dream she had, interrupting what I was doing. At first, I felt distracted by the E-mails and irritated by the interruption, but I made a conscious decision to listen. Immediately, I felt calmer. I realized how I had gotten a little stressed returning all the E-mails when I shifted my focus to listening to Michael. Contrary to what we might usually think about an interruption, that particular one allowed my whole morning to go more smoothly. Listening deeply is a conscious decision we can make and when we do, we receive the gift of calm.

## Caring and Compassion

Deep listening brings out the compassion and caring in us, because when we really understand another person, we see from their perspective why they behave and think the way they do. We see their innocence in being caught up in their fears and insecurities, just like we are. We see each other's humanness and our oneness when we listen deeply. All of us get caught up in the "reality" of our own thoughts, which leads to all of our problems and difficulties in life. However, when we are listening from our natural Self, we are connected to the natural Self of the other person. This connection allows us to see the common spirit of each of us.

Compassion is what happens when our heart is open while being with another person but without trying to change, fix, or otherwise rescue him or her. It also allows us to care for another person without bringing us down or taking on his problems as our own. Have you ever felt someone's compassion? It feels like a healing balm.

The old saying "There but for the grace of God go I" is the meaning of compassion. When we see another in pain, we are reminded of our own human frailty and vulnerability when we are unaware that our thinking is creating our experience. When we feel compassion for someone who is suffering, we don't judge the other person as inferior; instead, we see just how innocent human beings are in subjecting themselves to their own limited thinking. Pity, unlike compassion, has an element of superiority to it.

While compassion allows us to recognize another person's pain, it also allows us to see that pain as separate from ourselves. Therefore, we do not take on that person's pain as our own. In fact, compassion is like a psychological immunity to other people's pain and circumstances. On the other hand, sympathy can lead to commiseration, advice giving, and fixing, and that will bring us down.

Here is an example of the impact compassion can have. Jerry, a manager at a hospital, was in his office when one of his staff came in, apparently in an emotional upheaval. Jerry listened deeply to her, and at the end of a ten-minute conversation, the woman felt relieved and calm. She thanked Jerry, who had listened with a compassionate ear but given no advice. The woman realized her own solution just by having a good listening ear. Jerry had an impact on her, simply by remaining in his natural Self and seeing her innate health and natural ability to come up with solutions. That is the power of deep listening.

### Connected

Whenever I give a seminar and ask the participants to do a listening exercise (like the one in the box on page 64, "Listening as a Way of Life"), I am amazed at how quickly people feel connected to total strangers or even to people they have known a long time but didn't feel close to. When we listen deeply, our hearts open and we are in touch with true feelings of love and caring. We see past the defenses and external behavior to the true Self that is just like us. We see the common bond that connects us. I have seen hardened criminals in prison, who are taught Health Realization principles, learn to deeply listen, and I am struck by how close they become to each other and even to the guards. People of all races, ages, and nationalities feel oneness when they engage in deep listening. We can't truly listen deeply unless we are in the present moment and grounded in our true Self. The simple power of deep listening can heal a relationship or end a war. When we are our true Self, we are a healing agent and we extend timeless love that touches everyone. It is up to them to choose to receive this love.

The following illustration demonstrates our common connection through deep listening. When the ego-states of two people communicate, they see only their differences, but when they deeply listen from the natural Self, they see their common unity.

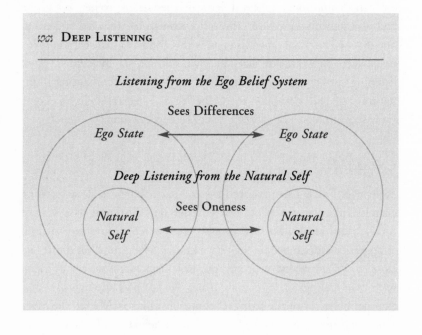

### ෴ DEEP LISTENING

*Listening from the Ego Belief System*

Sees Differences

*Ego State* ←——————→ *Ego State*

*Deep Listening from the Natural Self*

Sees Oneness

*Natural Self* ←——————→ *Natural Self*

## Communication

The last result of deep listening is that it creates true understanding among people, which is what communication is all about. Unfortunately, true understanding rarely occurs in our modern world because we don't know how to listen. We are so busy-minded and distracted that we don't live in the natural Self and therefore, we don't listen. The truth is, we can't afford to not listen. If people can communicate, they can begin to work together harmoniously, rather than against one another. True communication leads to a meeting of the minds; that is, our hearts and minds in unity. That, in turn, leads to cooperation, caring, teamwork, and connection.

Communication is often cited as the foundation of effective and harmonious relationships with our significant others. True communication is not a technique; it is the natural sharing of your true Self. At this level of sharing, you will experience a level of intimacy that is beyond your expectations—you will live at the speed of love.

# From Listening to Insight

Deep listening has many benefits, but one of the bonuses is that it connects us to our core of innate health and our source of insights. Have you ever noticed that when you have either deeply listened to someone or been listened to, the other person or you solve the problem?

When we listen deeply, we open the floodgates to the source of our own insights. When our thinking gets unstuck, we start to flow with new thoughts, thoughts that now seem obvious but that we couldn't see prior to the listening process. When we listen deeply, we are able to reflect, to step back from our crowded mind, and let in some fresh thinking. These insights can lead to healing of a person or a relationship.

## How Can Fear Block Deep Listening?

When we feel threatened and insecure, we stop listening with a clear and open mind. Instead, we fill our minds with all kinds of insecure thoughts. These thoughts involve three basic strategies:

1. To be right, to win
2. To be in control
3. To analyze, process, and intellectualize

Let's look at each of these strategies.

### *To Be Right, to Win*

Many people look at communication as a debate with one winner and one loser. The methods used to win are logic, reason, persuasion, manipulation, and threat. When we need to win or be right, we will not listen. To break this habit, we first need to see the possibility that every conflict can end in a win-win situation, if *both* parties deeply listen.

For example, a couple who were both lawyers had developed the habit through their work of being logical, manipulative, and analytical. This may be the common routine in the courtroom, but in their marriage it was disastrous. However, when they began to value listening, they saw it as a path to intimacy and more important than winning. Ironically, their communication improved without all the debate they had grown accustomed to.

The fear of not winning stems from the myth that there must be a winner and a loser. No one wants to be a loser, so we develop this stance as a way of self-preservation. This need to win is the work of the ego-self. When we are in the natural Self, we see that we are all connected, we are on the same team, and the solutions that will work for all of us are just not yet apparent. Opening ourselves up to this truth, coupled with deep listening, frees our mind to think creatively, to transcend the limitations of our thought system. Maslow called this "transcending the differences." In Chapter 9, "Transforming Conflict into Whole-hearted Resolution," I will go into depth about this model. When we are living from the natural Self, we are capable of this transcendent thinking that leads to breakthroughs and insights, and we are aware of how to create a win-win solution for both people.

## To Be in Control

Another form fear takes is the need to be in control. When we are in this state of mind, we anticipate all possible outcomes, rehearse our responses, and do everything we can to maintain the upper hand. Above all, our goal is to avoid appearing weak or vulnerable.

When we are afraid of losing control, what we are actually afraid of is the unknown. The ego-self is in control, and the natural Self is out of the picture. But when we trust in the unknown as friend rather than foe, we realize that solutions neither of us had ever considered could come at any moment. In trusting the unknown, we can relinquish control over the outcome. All fear is based on our separation from this one power—the true Self. When we forget that we are one with the Source, we feel fear. Clearing our mind and having faith in the unknown gives us an awareness of our true nature.

For example, a parent, not knowing what to say to a child, can just listen until something occurs to him from that inner source of wisdom.

The state of "not doing"—not trying to come up with something immediately and trusting instead that an appropriate response will come naturally—is what allows the answer to surface. Our need to be in control blocks any insights from our innate common sense. Slowing down to the speed of love requires the reflection of a quiet mind for an insight to surface.

## To Analyze, Process, and Intellectualize

The third form that fear may take is "analysis paralysis." The intellect can be a useful tool, but combined with fear it can be a deadly weapon. Some of the most intelligent people in history have been the perpetrators of the worst crimes against humanity—all based on their internal logic. Logic is internally consistent; that is, whatever assumptions you begin with, you can build a logical case for in your mind. People justify infidelity, violence, abuse, and deceit—all on internal logic.

When we get caught up in analyzing what a person is saying rather than just listening to what he is saying, we run the risk of judging and categorizing him. Having faith in the spiritual nature of the other person and in our own spiritual nature to give us feedback about whether the conversation is going toward balance or imbalance allows us to relax our grip on our intellect and deeply listen. The following is an illustration about the power of deep listening and presence from a man who was a professional analyzer and controller.

### A CEO Learns to Listen

Larry is the CEO of a large hospital. He is the epitome of organization, planning, and time management. He runs his hospital with a military-like efficiency. Larry hired me to help his staff reduce their stress and be able to think more clearly in a time of rapid change. He attended the first training session along with his other senior managers.

On the second day of the training, he returned to the class with this story: "I couldn't believe what happened last night. My wife and I were supposed to meet another couple for dinner and a play at 6:00. I knew my wife would be late because she always is, and I am always a stickler for punctuality. I called her about 5:30 to remind her of our 6:00 reservation, and I sensed her bristling at my pressuring her. It was at this moment that I realized I wasn't in the moment. As a matter of fact, I realized I rarely am, as I put punctuality ahead of enjoying each other. I decided that night to just listen and to be present with her. She was five minutes late, but I didn't care; I was just glad to see her. Instead of reciting a litany of our day's accomplishments, which is our habit, I decided to just listen and be with her. The other couple canceled at the last moment, which would have normally ruined my evening. Instead, I decided to see it as an opportunity for Sue and me to be together alone. We hadn't done that in a long time. We had the most pleasant night since we first fell in love. I can't believe how we have missed each other as we got caught up in the busy lives of our careers and raising a family. The time we never seemed to have was right under our noses once we slowed down to the speed of love."

Deep listening is one of the guidelines of finding timeless love. Deep listening heals, transforms, connects us, and helps us understand each other. When we take the time to really listen to each other, we make room for a meeting of the minds and a heart-to-heart connection.

In Chapter 7, I will talk about the ability to speak from the heart. When we combine listening deeply and speaking from the heart, we can have a communication that will keep our relationship growing. But first, I will talk about how we create our experience of life, in the next chapter on separate realities.

# 5

# SEPARATE REALITIES

*A human being is a part of the whole called by us "universe," a part limited in time and space. He experiences himself, his thoughts and feelings, as something separated from the rest, a kind of optical delusion of his consciousness. This delusion is a kind of prison for us. Our task must be to free ourselves from this prison by widening our circle of compassion to embrace all living creatures and the whole of nature in all its beauty. Nobody is able to achieve this completely but the striving for such achievement is in itself part of the liberation and a foundation for inner security.*

—ALBERT EINSTEIN

I USED TO THINK that we were all seeing the same reality. I believed that reality was "out there," and it was my life purpose to understand it accurately. Through listening to others, becoming informed, and studying books and other sources of information, I developed a thought system about life and called it *reality*.

When others didn't see life the way I did, I did one of two things: I judged myself and thought I must be stupid, uninformed, or naive; or I judged the other person as stupid, uninformed, or naive. The more I interacted with other people, the more confused and judgmental I became. "If they're right, I must be wrong and therefore not as intelligent." Or, "If I'm right, I'm better than they are, and they're all wrong." This way of thinking led to a great deal of disappointment, judgment, self-doubt, and conflict in my relationships.

I don't think I was much different from others in this regard. Most of us go through life in our own little worlds, not knowing that others don't see life as we do. We seek out people who are like-minded so we can be more sure that how we perceive the world is the truth. In looking for a mate, we often look for someone who sees life as we do. Ultimately, however, we are disappointed to learn that we don't see life the same at all times, and we then spend the rest of our relationships trying to convince our mates that they are wrong and we try to get them to see things our way. This approach leads to conflict, distance, anger, and frustration. In fact, it leads to much of the conflict of humankind.

In this chapter, I am going to show you a way out of this human dilemma.

What I didn't realize earlier in my life is that we are *all* living in a separate, individually thought-created reality. Each human being is born into the natural Self, and in this state, we are all in unity and see life in innocence and without judgment. Fill a room full with babies of all races, religions, nations, and backgrounds, and all you have is harmony—no judgment, prejudice, or conflict—just babies being babies. Fill the room with those same babies twenty years later and you might have conflict, arguments, or even war.

As we go through life, we form our view of reality—what is right or wrong, true or false, good or bad, and moral or immoral. What changes is that we move away from the natural Self and develop an ego-self. It is natural to bring forth our own unique expression into the world. This is what makes life interesting and varied. If we all thought the same, life would be boring.

However, when we believe that our way is the only correct way to think, we develop a lack of respect, love, and interest in others. Instead we feel alienated, alone, distant, and in conflict. The following diagram will illustrate the nature of separate realities. The arrows on the side indicate our level of consciousness or awareness. The profiles on the lower part of the diagram indicate our ego-self belief system. The pro-

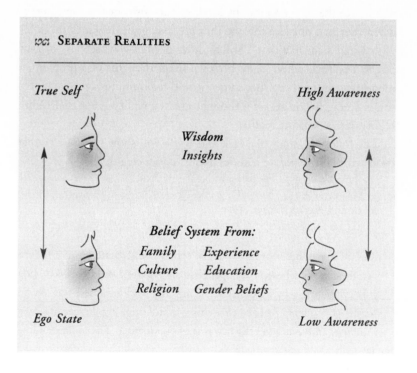

**SEPARATE REALITIES**

*True Self*

*High Awareness*

*Wisdom*
*Insights*

*Belief System From:*

| *Family* | *Experience* |
|----------|--------------|
| *Culture* | *Education* |
| *Religion* | *Gender Beliefs* |

*Ego State*

*Low Awareness*

files on the top part of the diagram indicate the clarity of thought that comes from a higher level of awareness, unimpeded by our personal thought system.

Until I gained an understanding about how we all create our reality, my life was full of stress and conflict. Once I realized how we design our experience of life, my relationships transformed. I felt more understanding, compassion, appreciation, and love. I realized how life is generated from the inside out.

For example, if I am driving down the road in my car with several other people, we will all be seeing, perceiving, and experiencing a different reality. Some will notice the plants, flowers, and trees. Others will notice the automobiles, the kinds of cars, how fast they are going, when they had one like the one they are seeing, or they may think, "I wish I had a car like that." Still another person won't see any of that but will be focused on his or her own inner thoughts of a problem, a memory, or something that someone said five minutes ago. Each person is seeing his or her own thought-created reality—not the "right" reality, just a separate reality.

The following story of Mark and Karla will show how one couple dealt with their separate realities about "closet cleanliness."

### Mark and Karla's Closet Story

Karla: I remember hearing about the concept of separate realities for the first time. It was a beacon of hope. I had always wondered what was wrong with Mark and why he didn't see things my way, because I was always "right." I suddenly realized that this was my thinking, he had his own thinking, and that was OK. It was very comforting. The understanding has truly saved our marriage. All the differences we have—male/female, neat/messy, frugal/extravagant—are no longer a big deal. The numerous arguments about all the little details that were insidiously eroding our marriage were replaced by understanding and a deep sense of connection. Before, we held grudges; resented each other; and judged each other as wrong, stupid, and out to make each other's lives miserable. We took everything very personally. When I see that my irritation is coming from my thinking and not him, it's easier to let it go and get back to the warm feelings we share with each other.

Mark: I was stuck in thinking, "Why doesn't she do things like me? Why can't she grasp my concepts? She's doing this to make my life miserable! She knows what is important to me, so she must have it in for me." I held lots of grudges that permeated my marriage.

For example, the closet. On the one side of the closet everything is very neat—the shoes all line up perfectly, the shirts are all hung up at equal distances apart. It looks perfect! On the other side of the closet, if you look up, you miss everything because it's *all* on the floor. For the longest time (twelve years), I thought she was doing this intentionally to make me mad. I never spoke to her about this for years, but I got angry about some other very insignificant detail and would blow up at her.

Karla: I had no idea that any of this was even an issue. The closet looked fine to me. I was raised in a small home with seven kids and it was always a mess—that was normal to me. So I never saw my mess in the closet. Mike was raised the opposite. In his home, cleanliness was next to godliness. Our separate realities collided in the closet!

Mark: It never occurred to me that she could be thinking differently than I did. If she loved me, she would pay attention to how I like to do things and would have done what I wanted. Once I realized that she thought differently and perceived the whole situation completely differently, I quit blaming her and just accepted her reality.

Karla: Once he let go of his resentment about my style, I began to try to clean up my side of the closet, though it still isn't like his. We just accept each other's style, and the heaviness is gone about the closet. Now when we do get upset about it, we know it is a signal that our mood has dropped. The closet situation is now a gift.

## The Source of All Experience

Mark and Karla's story shows us the power of understanding separate realities in a relationship. It points to the power of realizing the three principles in our lives. I too realized that literally *all* of my experience is created through the powers of Mind, Consciousness, and Thought. I realized this at a level of insight that was beyond mere intellectual understanding. I started to see that I was thinking and to realize the connection between this and the way I perceived any given circumstance. More fundamentally, I realized that I am the *creator* of my experience. This realization turned my life around 180 degrees.

As you read about these principles of how we create our experience of life, initially they may only be intellectual concepts for you. Whenever you learn anything that is new, your coach or teacher can only demonstrate, describe, model, or paint a picture of the desired outcome. You, as the receiver of this information, must *experience* what he or she is talking about. Read beyond the words and listen deeply to understand what they are pointing to. As you have your own insights, these words will come to life for you too.

Let's take a moment now to explain the principles behind all human behavior and experience.

## The Three Principles: Mind, Consciousness, and Thought

Three fundamental principles govern our experience. They are *Mind, Consciousness,* and *Thought.* How can three vague, abstract words give us practical solutions for our everyday life experience? They sound like something useful for a psychologist, philosopher, or maybe a monk, but how could they be of value for our lives or, more specifically, our relationships?

Principles underlying anything initially appear mysterious and hard to understand. However, from my first contact with them, I felt that I was hearing something I already intuitively knew on some level, but I had never heard it articulated before. I now see that on a deeper level, we do know these principles. They are written in our hearts and we now "remember" what our natural Self already knows. This inner wisdom is as natural to us as instincts (to migrate, give birth, and so on) are to animals. Whether we understand them or believe that they exist doesn't matter; we are still affected by them. Consider the law of gravity. We can't see it, many of us can't scientifically explain it, and yet none of that matters to gravity—we are still subject to its law. Most of us don't ignore gravity or try to misuse it, because we understand it through our direct experience. For instance, we would never step off the roof of a fourteen-story building. That would not be common sense, and we know the consequences would be disastrous.

It is my hope that through the stories and examples in this book, the principles of Mind, Consciousness, and Thought will come alive for you and no longer be three abstract words but practical, commonsense principles that you can trust and live by. I hope that you will begin to know them through your direct experience, which is the only way that they can truly be revealed. They are written in our hearts and they surface through remembering—we become aware of what already exists without having to learn it.

## Mind

Mind is very profound. It is the source of everything, including the principles of Consciousness and Thought. Without the principle of

Mind, the other two would not exist. Contrary to the way it is conventionally used, Mind is not localized in the brain. It is an invisible power that is the source of all that is. It is undetectable through our intellect or our senses, because it is invisible and without attributes. Fortunately, as spiritual beings, we can be aware of Mind, in that we are an extension of this universal source.

Universal Mind is like electricity. We can't see it, yet its power gives us light, propels our appliances, runs our computers, and heats our homes. It is invisible; it has no form or attributes, yet it becomes visible in the ways it is used. Without electricity, none of our electrical devices would be able to function. Like electricity, Mind powers us to experience all that we see, smell, hear, taste, and touch.

**UNIVERSAL AND PERSONAL MIND** Mind is universal. Just as we are all connected to the power plant for our electricity, each of us is one with the power of the Universal Mind. Some call this Universal Mind "God," some call it the "Brahman," and others call it the "Great Spirit," the "Force," "Love," or the "Energy" of all things. It doesn't really matter what you call it, as long as you know that it exists. Through our free will, we can use our personal mind to create any life we can imagine or think up. However, we can never lose our connection to the Universal Mind. When we acknowledge it, we recognize the source of all that is seen and unseen.

Knowing that a larger force exists is the cornerstone of Health Realization principles. When we falsely depend on the ego, we are trapped in time-bound love and have only our personal memory and intellect to guide us. With timeless love, we are connected to the Universal Mind/Intelligence and are thus able to function freely—to flow with our creative thinking, the deeper intelligence of wisdom. When our thinking is guided by the deeper intelligence of Mind, it uses all the information stored in our memory, but it uses it with understanding and insight.

Timeless love is the core of each one of us. Creating healthy relationships starts with the willingness to look within and make the choice to rejoin this core that is the natural Self. Timeless love is the essential ingredient that heals pain and resentments in relationships and it is the source of constant regeneration.

With our personal mind and free will, we use the powers of Mind, Thought, and Consciousness to create our own personal version of "reality," including our idea of who we are in this "reality." We can create this personal version from the illusion of separation or from the awareness of unity. This is the principle in action.

We have unknowingly created, through a thought of separation from our spiritual source, our ego-self. We then create our own personal, illusionary version of "reality," including our idea of who we are in this milieu. I use the word *illusionary* in the sense that we are seeing reality through the thought-created perceptional filter of separation, not the true spiritual reality—Love.

However, if we remain aware that we are one with our spiritual source, then we are living from the natural Self rather than the ego-self. We still create our own personal version of reality, including our idea of who we are within it, but it is not compromised by the illusion of separation. I still use the word *personal* here in the sense that although we are the same as Mind, each of us expresses this source differently—we are an individuation of Mind.

From the natural Self, we can relate to each other on the foundation of our *sameness* in spirit and also appreciate our unique expressions of this Spirit; in short, we enjoy our differences! What a harmonious and satisfying way to be in relationships.

If we recognize that Mind is the source of everything, and if we understand that each of us is one with that source, then our lives would certainly change not only in a profound way, but in a practical way as well. We could relax in the knowledge that we have an all-present, all-powerful, all-knowing resource to guide and direct us.

We would recognize that the source of love is also Mind. In addition, when we lack a feeling of love, we would know that it hasn't gone anywhere, but is within us always. So much of our frenetic pace of living is driven by this unconscious gnawing thought that we are alone. When we slow down to the speed of love, we reconnect to our true, natural Self, and our feelings of loneliness disappear.

## Consciousness

Consciousness is the invisible quality that allows us to be aware of existence. It is Mind expressing itself as life. Consciousness is our individual experience of Mind, the very core of our existence. Like Mind, Consciousness is totally neutral; that is, it is neither positive nor negative, good nor bad, healthy nor unhealthy—it just "is."

Pure Consciousness is pure awareness—awareness that everything is in union with Mind. How consciously we live depends on the *level of our awareness*. As we become more conscious, we live more as our natural Self, always in union with Mind—the source of love.

Through Consciousness, we sense, feel, observe or perceive, and act—that is how we experience the gift of life. To what level we experience this gift of life, as I said earlier, depends on how conscious or aware we are. For instance, if we are living at the level of our ego-self, we are not conscious of our union with Mind—we are not conscious of the natural Self. Our interpretations of life and our relationships, our perception of our mate—all will be skewed by our lack of awareness. Yet the principle of Consciousness remains the same; it is how conscious or aware we are that makes a difference in our experience.

In its purity, Consciousness is always clear and is always reflecting Mind. Because pure Consciousness reflects Mind, this innate intelligence is all-knowing, all-present, and all-powerful. If we understood the immense capability of pure Consciousness and trusted it, if we were to surrender to its all-knowing power, we would see that within our consciousness is inspiration that is responsive to our every need, and custom-designed from moment to moment for our lives. We must be willing to trust our deeper nature, however, to experience these results.

We are not always open to experiencing and relying upon our natural Self, the extension of pure Consciousness, as an all-knowing resource that will guide and direct us. Why not? Because from the moment we were born, we were taught to look outside ourselves for what we need. We were taught that external things would make us happy, complete, successful, and more. The flip side of that coin is that we were taught that other people or circumstances can make us sad, mad, and so on. We become prisoners of our belief systems and lost in our separate versions of realities. We don't realize that to see clearly, we have to let go of our ego thoughts (conditioned habits of thinking) that we use to try to control our lives. We have yet to realize that the true source of our experience is our use of the powers of Mind, Consciousness, and Thought.

From the time that we began looking outside for happiness and seeing ourselves as separate, our game of life took on the form of fulfilling our wants, needs, and desires. Gradually, we lost touch with our spiritual consciousness and began to go through life without the experience of trusting our spiritual guidance system. Our level of consciousness or awareness dropped.

Because Consciousness is awareness, it brings to life every thought we have. This is true regardless of whether our consciousness reflects the Universal Mind or the limitations of our ego-based beliefs. Consciousness gives us a total experience of our thoughts—we see and perceive our thoughts as reality. Although the reality we experience is our personal reality rather than an absolute reality, we are often unaware that we are creating our experience of reality through thought. We are to our thoughts like a fish is to water. In other words, we are as unaware that we are swimming in the reality of our thoughts, as a fish is unaware that it is swimming in water. Thought is so all-inclusive that our senses, our emotions, even our endorphins and our blood pressure—every part of us, visible or invisible—reflects the quality of the thought we are having at any given moment. If we mistake a stick for a snake, we're scared. If we think our wife or husband is inconsiderate, we're mad.

At low levels of understanding about life, Consciousness still brings us the experience of our thinking. The difference between a high level of understanding and a low level is that at the latter, we just aren't aware that we are using Consciousness to create our experience. At low levels of awareness, reality appears to be coming from "out there"—other people, circumstances, the weather, or any other type of external condition. Consciousness instantaneously brings each thought into our experience as what appears as an outside reality. This is the trap of our separate reality at a lower level.

For example, when Mark, the subject of the earlier story, would drop into a low mood, he would notice how messy Karla's side of the closet was, and he would become irritated. His whole demeanor would change, and he would spread this negativity to his relationship with his wife and two daughters. His thoughts were creating his experience, via Consciousness, but it looked like his experience was coming from the messy closet or his wife's intentions. As his level of consciousness began to go up, he would have the same habitual reaction to the messy closet but would quickly realize that the source of the experience was his own thinking. The closet became a barometer of his mood and a source of humor. Now Mark and Karla are very lighthearted about the closet when it comes up—all because they have realized the power of Thought and Consciousness to create their experience.

As we gain more understanding of life (wisdom), our level of consciousness rises, and we are more aware of how Thought creates our reality. As our level of awareness of the source of our experience goes up, we place less blame on the outside for our lives and see more of a connection between our unique experience of life and our powers of Mind, Thought, and Consciousness.

## *Thought*

Pure Thought is a power, a gift. Contrary to how we normally define thought, the principle of Thought, like Mind, is not localized in the brain. It is not the mental chatter of a busy mind or that continual conversation you may experience in your head. The power of Thought is the power to create form out of nothing. Like Mind and Consciousness, Thought is totally neutral. Every emotion, every action, every invention, everything in life derives from a thought.

Thought can come from the natural Self or from the ego-self. Thought that comes directly from the natural Self rises from a union with Mind. We call these thoughts "wisdom," "common sense," "inspiration," "insight," "creativity," "original thought," and "out-of-the-blue" thoughts. Thoughts that come from the ego-self are tainted by a belief system based on separation rather than the awareness of unity. We have the power to think anything we choose—this is the nature of free will. The quality of our thinking will indicate whether it is coming from the pure Thought of our natural Self or the contaminated thought of our ego-self.

So how can the principle of Thought make a difference in our lives and relationships? I used to feel like a victim of my past, other people, my finances, events, and other life circumstances. As a result, I would hold whomever I was in a relationship with responsible for all of my emotions, positive or negative. However, when I saw the connection of my experience to my own thinking, a huge burden was lifted. I felt free. I also felt responsible, but not guilty. I could see my habits of thinking as innocent and just part of my conditioned ego-self. We've all had a conditioned personal mind with all the good, bad, and ugly habits and experiences that come with life.

Fortunately, like a spring that is constantly pouring forth water, the true nature of our mind is for thoughts, positive or negative, to continually flow unobstructed. The more we are aware of our true spiritual nature, the more positive and/or insightful our thoughts. The less aware we are, the busier-minded and more possibly negative our thoughts become. Because the nature of our mind is to flow, I know that if I don't like my experience, it can change in an instant—as my thinking changes—without any effort on my part. Knowing that this is the natural state of our mind is helpful. This knowledge frees me from taking myself (or each thought) too seriously.

Because we have been unaware of our mind's flowing nature, we have blocked this natural process with mental chatter and created an obsession with thinking. We innocently try to "think" our way in and out of situations; we try to figure out life and consequently block the natural flow of insights that are available to guide us.

It was a great relief to me when I realized that I didn't have to "do" anything to have insights—the power of "true" Thought was within me. I discovered that it was more about "not doing" than doing. That is, the more I didn't try to figure out my life and my relationship and didn't constantly process my thinking, then the more easily my thoughts flowed. My mind quieted down. With these "thinking" blocks removed, insights and feelings of love easily surfaced from within my true nature. I felt increased peace, all my relationships began to flourish, and I received an added bonus—I had more time.

How does that work? When you are not engaging your ego-thought system in trying to figure out everybody and everything, your mind becomes clear. Like the analogy of the glass of water with the sediment at the bottom from Chapter 2, you can see "what is" from the wisdom of your natural Self. Although a busy mind gives the illusion of being productive, constant processing takes a lot of time, whereas an insight is timeless.

When we discover the source of Thought within us, we surrender to that Source, and "true" thoughts begin to come to us. These thoughts have a different quality from thoughts from the separated ego-self. Sometimes, it feels like a knowing or a certainty—it may be about an ordinary situation or it may be a profound insight about the understanding of life.

We've all had moments of clear thoughts from the natural Self; some we have recognized, and some we haven't trusted. Pure Thought from the natural Self is wholehearted in the sense that our mind and our heart are joined together in union with Mind. It is the way of coming to know this union of Universal Love. These thoughts are unselfish; they would never do harm, because they are connected to the Whole.

How do I notice that I am thinking and creating my experience? It seems difficult, given that most of our thinking seems to be out of our awareness. Fortunately, we have been blessed with a perfect inner guidance system—our true feelings and emotions. The quality of our feelings and emotions instantly informs us of the quality of our thinking and whether it is coming from our natural Self or the ego-self.

In the next chapter, we will take an in-depth look at our emotional guidance system, how we naturally go up and down in our awareness of our thinking, and whether we are in the natural Self or ego-self.

## The Three Principles and Separate Realities

When we understand and realize the power of the three principles to create our inner experience of life, we realize that everyone else is doing the exact same thing. Whether our thoughts are from the natural Self or our ego-self, they create our personal reality from moment to moment, and we bring that reality to life with consciousness.

Through the power of Mind, Thought, and Consciousness, we are all creating our experience from moment to moment. Once we create a thought, either from the natural Self or the ego-self, a chain reaction takes place, as shown in the following diagram. We have a thought—

it may be an observation or a perception. That perception could bring about an emotion, which would lead to a particular behavior, prompting a reaction. Together, these links in the chain form our experience of life—our separate reality.

Here is another example of the three principles and separate realities in action. If my wife is speaking to me and I am listening to her through the filter of my personal thinking, I will hear echoes of the past times she has said similar things, and I will erroneously conclude that she is saying the same thing now. If, however, I clear my mind and listen deeply in this moment, I will hear her afresh and perhaps accurately for the first time. I will gain a new appreciation for what she is

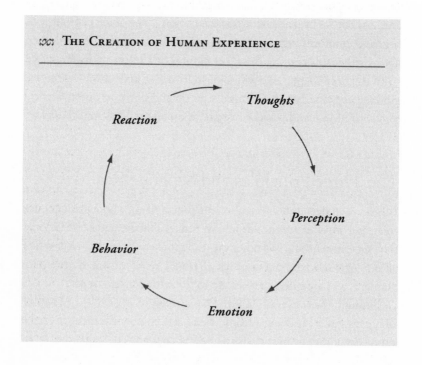

### ⋙ The Creation of Human Experience

Thoughts

Reaction

Perception

Behavior

Emotion

saying, or I might hear something totally new. I may even transcend her words and hear something much deeper in what she is saying that will take our relationship to a new level of closeness.

## We Are Already Complete

An understanding of these three principles of human experience brings new depth to the first guideline of timeless love: love is within. We are not lacking in love: we are already complete. We already possess the treasure we are seeking to find. As human beings, we are part of a whole that is all-knowing, all-loving, and infinite. In other words, we are spiritual beings. This means that we are more than meets the eye (as well as the other senses). We are more than our behavior, our emotions, our personality, and our bodies. We are the consciousness and the life force that creates all of our experience of the world and of ourselves, on a moment-to-moment basis. We are the same as Mind, as well as an individual expression that I have referred to as the *natural Self*.

Because we are this spiritual nature, we possess everything that we could ever want, need, or desire, including love, happiness, peace of mind, abundance, and perfect health. Full accomplishment is our true nature. In psychology, we have referred to this ability to fulfill our potential as *resilience*. Resilience is the quality of human beings to return to health, to adapt, to recover from hurt and loss, and to fall back in love when we have lost the feeling. It is what explains how people heal from illness, trauma, troubled relationships, and adverse circumstances. It also explains the infinite capacity of human beings to create new things, ideas, and realities. In the natural ecology of the earth, an ocean, a river, and a forest all have an amazing capacity to rejuvenate when they are damaged through storms, fires, pollution, and other disasters. We too have that capacity for continuous healing and renewal.

Most of us don't think of ourselves as resilient. We have been taught that we are sinners, genetically predisposed to certain maladies, incomplete and in need of education, weak, lacking in talent, or that we have undeveloped potential. In other words, we have been taught, and we believe, that we need a lot of improvement. We seek this improvement in education, religion, self-help programs, diets, workout programs, psychotherapy, or self-analysis—anything we believe will give us what we are lacking. This belief that we are incomplete and need fixing may be the biggest error we have made in the past centuries. It teaches us to not rely on the natural Self, but strive toward self (ego) improvement. We run on the treadmill of life trying to catch up to the illusion that something is missing.

You may wonder how I can be so certain that we are already complete and possess everything we could ever need, especially in light of the present state of our world, which is full of disease, psychological dysfunction, greed, war, and poverty. When you truly look within, you will discover all the answers you seek. You will discover wisdom, your true Self, and you will discover love.

# The Implications of the Principles for Relationships

When we understand the principles, we become wise. We start to use these powers and gifts more intelligently. If I know that my thinking can influence the experience of my day, I may ignore certain thoughts and let them go, and others I may take to heart, depending on what is appropriate in the moment. For example, when I am caught up in a reaction to my mate, I will see that reaction as stemming from my thoughts, and the situation won't become an issue of blame for either party. Rather than reject and bury my emotions or blame the "outside" for my reaction, I can let my thoughts flow, to be replaced by healthier thoughts. If I need to understand anything about this reaction, I will have an insight as to what my reaction was about when I return to my natural Self.

In my relationship, my understanding of the three principles has shown me that how much love I am experiencing at any given moment is a direct result of my level of awareness of my natural Self, not of what my mate says or does—no matter what her behavior is. If I have a judgment about her, it's obvious where my experience is coming from. Forgetting this has led to many an argument and unpleasant experience in my life. But when I am aware of the source of my experience, I can acknowledge my thinking, step back, and look again with new eyes. When I regain my perspective, I relax and see what is before me with compassion, new appreciation, or whatever is the appropriate response. I am able to understand that I am seeing life from my separate reality and that it may not coincide with how another sees life.

Realizing the power and all-pervasiveness of the principles in our lives leads to a very profound conclusion—no one can make me happy or unhappy. In fact, nothing in the outer world has that power. When my experience is from my natural Self, it will be one of timeless love, and I will observe life in a wise manner. When I am caught up in my ego-self, I will project out from my belief system, and I will experience the separation of time-bound love.

Of course, sometimes your initial reaction will be a hurt or angry thought; that is quite human, especially in the case of a partner's transgression. However, knowing that thought is the source of your experience allows you to choose whether or not to continue with painful thoughts. I am not suggesting that you deny or stuff your emotions; I am suggesting that you let your thoughts flow, so as to access your deeper wisdom. Some people stay angry or hurt for an instant and then let it go. Others hang on to the thought and the emotion for days, weeks, months, years, or indefinitely—ruining their relationships and their mental health in the process. Once your mind is in a nonreactive state, you can more clearly see what to do in any situation. In an emotionally reactive state, your judgment and common sense can often be clouded.

It is important to just accept any emotions that you are having, without judging yourself. This will help to quiet your mind and bring you back to the balance of your natural Self. When one comes from a nonreactive state, what may have been an angry emotional reaction would then become, if appropriate, firm *resolve*. One would have the clarity of a calm mind along with the appropriate resolution to make the necessary changes. I will speak on emotions and feelings in greater depth in Chapter 6.

The more we understand the three principles and the way we create our lives, the more joy we will feel, the more love we will experience, the wiser we will be, the more freedom we will have—we will slow down to the speed of love. Throughout this book I will be referring to the principles, because they form the foundation of understanding that can lead to loving, realizations, and healthy relationships.

# 6

# NAVIGATING RELATIONSHIPS: LISTENING TO OUR FEELINGS

❡◦——◦❡

FROM MOMENT TO MOMENT, we are constantly creating our experience of reality through the powers of Mind, Consciousness, and Thought. Now how do we use that information to navigate through the ebb and flow of relationships? The short answer is through our feelings and emotions.

Our feelings, sensations, and emotions are information about the *quality* of experience we are creating at each moment. They are neither "good" nor "bad"; they are simply information. Every thought we have creates a reverberation of energy through the body—electrical, biochemical, and neurological. In other words, we experience our creation of reality through our physical body as sensations. The quality of those sensations alerts us to the quality of our thinking. They inform us of how we are using Thought and Consciousness to create our lives.

Many people are so estranged from their feelings and their bodies that they are unaware of the feedback mechanism that is available to them as a guidance system. I've had clients who don't even know when they are experiencing *any* discomfort. I've stopped them in the middle of an emotional rant of anger and blame and asked them if they were reacting, and they replied, "No, I'm not reacting, I feel fine." As I inquire further about what they are sensing in their body, they gradually realize their body is full of sensations that they had never noticed. This denial applies not only to feelings and emotions, but even sensations of physical pain and illness. As a culture, many of us see this denial as a sign of strength, to block out awareness of all sensations to be strong, successful, and survive in life.

The exercise on the following page is one that I do in all my seminars to help participants begin to "hear" the language of feelings and emotions in their bodies. They are often surprised to notice how their body responds to a change in thought immediately and also how clearly distinct each feeling and emotion is experienced in their body. Do this exercise before you continue reading and the rest of the chapter will make more sense.

# Feelings and Emotions: Our Built-In Guidance System

Both feelings and emotions are essential parts of our built-in guidance system. Each alerts us to listen to our Self. Although feelings and emotions come from very different levels of consciousness, they are both

## ∞ AWARENESS OF OUR SENSATIONS

Take a moment now to be aware of your body's sensations. In your mind, conjure up your idea of the sensation of anxiety. Once you have a memory or image that creates anxiety, observe your body's sensations. Notice any change in muscle tension, heart rate, breathing, and discomfort. Don't try to change it or judge it, just notice it. Now, conjure up your idea of the sensation of gratitude; again, notice the body's sensations. How do the two sensations differ in the body?

useful for navigating through our lives and our relationships. To make the best use of our feelings and emotions, it is important to understand what they are, how feelings and emotions differ from one another, and how they can help us slow down to the speed of love.

### *The Difference Between Emotions and True Feelings*

Although most people refer to their emotions as "feelings," a true feeling is direct information from the natural Self. True feelings are the pure or true thoughts that I referred to in the previous chapter. However, they are not what we commonly define as thought. Generally we consider thought as coming to us in the more obvious form of language, such as the inner dialogue in our heads. True feelings are thoughts at a more subtle level, before they take the form of language. They are the intelligence of the natural Self. This spiritual intelligence, which is the principle of Consciousness in the physical body, stimulates thoughts and sensations that guide us in every situation. We sometimes refer to these sensations as "gut feelings," "instincts," "intuition," or a "knowing." We will talk more later in this chapter about how to recognize these sometimes subtle signals.

Understanding emotions is also an all-important component of listening to our built-in guidance system. Many people believe that their emotions are the "real" thoughts of their hearts. Others believe that if someone is emotional, whatever that person says should be immediately discounted. Neither is true. However, I hope to bring a clearer picture to this much-misunderstood subject and show how awareness of our emotions plays an important part in using our built-in guidance system.

Emotions are *not* from the same source as a true feeling, but nevertheless, they are part of our guidance system. Because most people use the terms *feelings* and *emotions* interchangeably, I have defined a true feeling as the spiritual intelligence of the natural Self. Emotion is defined by *Webster's Universal Dictionary* as "any strong agitation of the feelings actuated by experiencing love, fear, et cetera, and usually accompanied by certain physiological changes such as increased heartbeat or respiration."

When a child is born, one might wonder, what is this blissful experience we feel? Or, when someone we care deeply about tells us he or she loves us, do we feel an emotion or a true feeling? I would say what we experience is a true feeling, and, at that moment, we are one with our spiritual nature. When we respond from timeless love, we feel love, gratitude, joy, compassion, or whatever is appropriate for each situation. If we feel agitation, even in a positive feeling, it would be an emotion.

Emotions and thoughts from our ego's belief system can block the stillness needed to listen to the wisdom of our hearts, but through observation we can use them as a barometer of our thinking. If we have an emotional reaction from our belief system, it is a red flag that tells us that our mind is not quiet enough to receive an insight. The sensation of moving away from balance tells us to let go of our present thinking, let our thoughts flow, and trust in our innate health to bring us the solution. Wisdom is found underneath an emotion, but to harvest it we must have a quiet mind.

A quiet mind does not denote a dull mind. If we live amid a flurry of busy thinking from our belief system that is seemingly positive, it may be better than negative thinking but it is still a busy mind and not in alignment with the natural Self. Some people often mistake excitement for true feelings. They like the adrenaline rush and think that life would be dull without it. For them, excitement may be the only "positive" feeling they have much experience with. Once they experience what it feels like to live from their true nature, they are more readily aware of the differences. They realize what they before thought might be dull is instead a natural passion for living. When they are experiencing the true feelings of the natural Self, they are uninterested in looking outside for fulfillment in the "caffeine-rush feeling" that excitement contains.

When we are caught up in the reality of the separated self, we try to protect ourselves and those close to us. Consequently, we can react emotionally to perceived threats and project our defensive thoughts onto a person or situation, warranted or not. Sometimes, beneath that emotion, lies a true feeling, an insight that we have not yet listened to. We may have unknowingly pushed aside our wisdom so many times that our emotions have built to a high pitch.

Whether your emotion is loud because your perception is negative and you are going in a negative direction with your thinking, or your emotions are mounting because you are not listening to a true feeling, the remedy is still the same. Only a quiet mind can receive an insight. So how do we quiet our thinking in the midst of an emotional reaction?

### Acceptance: The Key to a Clear Mind

Acceptance is needed to move to stillness and to discern the grain of truth in our feelings or emotions. It is a much-overlooked component in the letting-go process that I will now describe. To rejoin the natural Self, we first have to truly accept whatever phase, mood, or level of consciousness we are experiencing at that given moment. That doesn't mean that we accept the negative emotion as a way to be; it means we lovingly accept ourselves. It means we accept that we are having those thoughts; it doesn't mean that we are those thoughts.

When you refrain from defending, explaining, or rejecting and let go of any judgment you have about yourself or others, your head will soon clear and allow an insight to surface. Notice what it feels like when you accept yourself completely—it takes the pressure off. This is *self-forgiveness*. It immediately wipes the slate clean for you to begin again. Until you are able to accept where you are at that moment, you will not be able to let go of your thinking. Until you let go of your thinking, your mind will not disengage and return to stillness. Until you return to the stillness of the natural Self, you will not have the insights that will guide you in your life. This is how our built-in guidance system works.

# Navigating Our Ups and Downs

In the world of relationships, our emotions and feelings are as important to navigating our ups and downs as the instrument panel is to a pilot flying in low visibility. Feelings and emotions are navigational signals that can guide us to live from the natural Self and stay in the moment. When we understand these signals, we know when to ignore the perceptions that we have created from the ego-self. We see how to avoid the pitfalls of living in the past or future, and we know how to avoid being influenced by an old memory. These perceptions of reality are actually illusions that keep us trapped in the circular thinking of the ego.

## Decoding Emotions and Feelings

When we overanalyze or pick apart a true feeling, we cover up our inner intelligence with thoughts from our personal belief system. We label, define, and interpret our feeling sensations as "anger," "fear," "love," or "dislike," thus missing the grain of truth or pure thought contained in the sensation. At other times, we simply experience an emotion that is the direct result of an association or a triggering of emotion from our conditioned, habitual self. For example, we may have an emotional reaction to hearing a song, watching a movie, or even being with someone else who is experiencing an intense emotion. In the latter case, we have a sympathetic response to that person's emotion.

Regardless of whether we are experiencing a true feeling or an emotion, we must see each as part of the instrument panel of our guidance system. For example, a feeling of discomfort, which we label as irritation, may be telling us that we are simply tired or hungry and need to rest or eat. Or the irritation is letting us know that something is out of balance in our relationship and we need to reflect on it or talk to the other person about it. Additionally, the same feeling that we have labeled "irritation" can be telling us that our mood is off and to just be quiet and listen to what we need. (We will talk more of moods in Chapter 9.) In the latter case, the irritation alerts us that we have moved out of balance with the natural Self. The true feeling, without the label of "irritation," is raw data that simply reminds us to listen and reflect. It needs only our respect and awareness to provide the guidance it was intended to give us.

Unfortunately, we often act on an emotional interpretation of our feelings without a moment's reflection, only to find out later that we have projected our own state of mind onto another person or situation.

The diagram below indicates how our emotions and feelings can let us know in which direction we are moving: toward the balance of the natural Self, or toward the imbalance of the ego-self.

In the story of the couple in the previous chapter, Mark and Karla had an issue about the cleanliness of the closet. Once Mark realized the power of his thinking to create his experience, the closet became a barometer of his moods, an indicator of how balanced or unbalanced he was. Whenever he noticed that the closet was bugging him, he knew his mood was off; he was leaning toward the unbalanced state of the ego-self. This habit of taking Karla's messiness personally always occurred when his mood was down and his level of awareness low. However, whenever his mood was up, he saw the messy side of her closet as neutral. It was neither a sign of disrespect nor a way to "get him"; it was simply her innocent habit.

---

### ∞ OUR NAVIGATIONAL COMPASS

| BALANCE | IMBALANCE |
|---|---|
| Love | Fear |
| Acceptance | Stubbornness |
| Calmness | Stress |
| Compassion | Judgment |
| Connectedness | Loneliness |
| Unity | Separation |
| Joy | Excitement |

*Natural Self* ⟵⟶ *Ego-Self*

## True Feelings or Conditioned Emotions

True feelings from our natural Self are unconditional; that is, they occur spontaneously, regardless of circumstances. Emotions that arise from our ego-self are based on conditioning, in which we are really responding to our own learned patterns of thinking rather than the other person or the circumstance.

For example, when I met the woman who would become my wife, my ego-self emotions were very conflicted. "She isn't my type." "She sure is intriguing." "Don't get hurt again." She sure is pretty." "This will never work." All of these contrasting thoughts led to emotions of fear leading to attraction leading to fear leading to attraction. However, my natural Self knew instantly that she was the "one." My natural feelings were uncontaminated by my past hurts, beliefs, judgments, and other prejudices. In my heart I knew I had found my life mate. My fear and insecurity weren't so sure.

Let me say a word about fear. Fear can be the voice of our common sense responding to real and present danger, as in the body's "fight-or-flight" mechanism, which is designed to move us to action. It can also be a response to the thought of *imagined* danger based on our past conditioning or memories—for example, fear of rejection because of a hurtful relationship in the past. One fear response leads to helpful action, the other impedes our healthy, commonsense action.

An analogy for dealing with fear is the instrument panel of our car. Sometimes a bell may go off, alerting us to pay attention to the instrument panel. Fear, like the bell, is there to get our attention so that we will further investigate the reason for the signal. In the car analogy, we wouldn't make assumptions or jump to conclusions as to why the bell rang; we would simply look to see if we are running low on gas, need an oil change, or if our seat belt needs to be fastened. In a relationship situation, fear alerts us to "look," to reflect from our true Self. If we reflect from a quiet mind, we will see clearly whether our fear is information from the present moment or past habitual thinking from our distorted belief system.

In my situation with Michael, whenever I imagined all the worst-case scenarios, I would want to avoid calling her. However, when my mind was calm, I could clearly hear the voice of my natural Self and I would want to take our relationship a step further (by calling her).

My ego-self continued to have the upper hand for several weeks, but my heart finally won out. Fortunately, I trusted it enough to listen to what it was telling me.

Let me share another example of how we inadvertently silence the true feelings of the natural Self.

### Setting Limits

A friend of mine, a widow named Susan, lives in a friendly little neighborhood. Her elderly neighbor, a man who was recently widowed and fifty years older, began to make advances toward her. It immediately made Susan feel very uncomfortable and annoyed that he would approach her on that level of interaction. She and her children had had a neighborly and close relationship with him and his wife for years. She thought of them as friends and grandparent figures, so this new development completely caught her off guard.

Although the neighbor's advances were blatant, the scenario didn't fit with Susan's belief system. And so she talked herself out of her true feelings and intuition. Her ego-self would say something like this: "I'm just reading into this. He's like a grandfather to me; he couldn't be 'hitting' on me."

Susan had a good awareness of the principle of Thought and how her thinking gave her an experience of reality, but this time, like many of us, she couldn't trust the subtle nuances of her gut feelings without hesitation.

Her inner voice of judgment kept getting in the way. Instead, her ego-self would insist, "You need to quit being so negative and judgmental of him. Be patient and compassionate. He's just a lonely old man."

In a sense, she was right. He was a lonely old man and deserving of compassion, as we all are, but "trying" to think compassionate thoughts doesn't work—it is still thinking that comes from the ego.

This type of thinking doesn't always appear to come from our ego-based belief system, especially when it presents the "humanitarian" theme or the "I should be more positive" theme. Nevertheless, Susan's feeling was her clue to listen deeply to herself. Susan was now approaching a new awareness and soon began to see the difference between what she labeled a negative thought and what was *neutral* information from a true feeling.

As her neighbor's advances persisted and became more inappropriate, she became very conflicted and confused about how to handle this situation. At one point, she called my wife and told her what was going on. Michael immediately said, "Susan, it sounds like you aren't listening to yourself—your feeling is telling you what to do." It was obvious that Susan was uncomfortable because the neighbor was inappropriately crossing her boundaries. Susan's feelings were shouting at her to set some clear boundaries, and she was not responding to that feeling.

Michael realized that Susan had a belief about "being compassionate and kind," and that belief was getting in the way of her common sense and instinctual feelings about what to do. Susan understood and realized that she had been blocking her true feelings so that she wouldn't appear "unloving."

Susan's reaction to her feeling was one of anger and annoyance. Someone else's reaction in the same situation may have been entirely different. They may have interpreted the feeling as fear, pity, frustration—the variety is endless. It is important to note that when we add our personal judgment on top of our true feelings we confuse the issue at hand. This is a very strong habit in human beings but easily remedied. We can bypass our confusion by accepting ourselves, honoring our feelings, and knowing that our insights will appear. Don't try to "figure out" what your feeling is telling you; it will show itself.

Susan finally did have a talk with her neighbor in a firm, yet kind manner. This talk didn't quite sink in with him, and she had to become more direct. She told him she couldn't have any contact with him because he couldn't respect her wishes. By listening to her deeper feelings of the heart (her spiritual Self), she protected herself and offered her neighbor a lesson in boundaries.

When we try to control our feelings instead of listening to them, we block the grain of truth that lies within them. Like a river, our feelings are flowing naturally, coming and going, as is appropriate to each moment. But when a true feeling goes against the belief system of the ego-self, we block that feeling in some way, as did Susan (denial, rationalization, intellectualization, suppression, or projection). We dam up the flowing river, and when we do, the river clogs up with unacknowledged, inexperienced emotions. These emotions become the sediment that blocks our clear thinking—wisdom and common sense. This blocking and ignoring of true feelings causes all the suffering and disease we experience in this life. Feelings are like a best friend; we need to accept them as they are so that they can tell us their truths.

# Denying and Projecting Feelings and Emotions

No feelings or emotions are inherently bad. However, knowing this doesn't give us permission to act on our emotions, but simply allows us to pause to have the discernment of wisdom to act appropriately. When we try to control our true feelings, it is because we don't understand them. Their meaning is unknown to us. It can be helpful to realize that emotions are not true feelings, but rather a *response* to a true feeling. Our emotional responses may be from fear or from love. For example, if we choose to hang on to our limited thinking we may respond to our true feelings with a fearful emotion. Universal Love is the innate source of a true feeling. If we are emotionally moved while listening deeply to our true feeling, then that response would be from love.

Within the ego-self, we may respond to our deeper feelings with fear. Why? Because the deeper feeling threatens the very life of the ego-self—the internal logic of our belief/thought system. We try to control what we don't want to know. We innocently form concrete opinions and beliefs to replace the natural process of our inner guidance system. When we form and rely upon an opinion to give us an answer, it blocks us from seeing life new in the present moment. Our opinions become solid and rigid. So, for us to maintain our opinion as "truth," we have to push aside our true feelings.

## Fear: The Response of the Separated Self

When we are separated from our spiritual core and from the spiritual core of others, we experience fear. In the fearful ego-self, we don't know what to do with the information that is coming to us in the form of sensations of true feelings, so what do we do with them? We do one of two things:

1. We deny our true feelings and push them out of our awareness.
2. We judge our feeling, and thus distort it; then we project our self-created emotion onto others or outside situations.

DENIAL When we feel something that goes against our belief system, we reject or push aside those feelings, but they do not go out of our consciousness; they just go out of our awareness. They become invisible to us.

Sometimes we deny our emotions because they are unacceptable to us or too uncomfortable to experience. Other times, we become attached to emotions, such as self-pity, resentment, sadness, or jealousy, because we have grown accustomed to them. We may hang on to these emotions so that we don't have to face a deeper truth. These habits are all examples of the ego-self at work, because the natural Self accepts, listens to, and embraces all that we feel. When it does, it gathers the much-needed information that comes with the feeling in the form of insights, common sense, and good decisions.

As a child, I was very sensitive to my emotions and to the feelings of others, animals, and even nature. I was teased for being overly sensitive and told I wasn't being a man. Eventually, I grew numb to my true feelings to survive my surroundings. In my innocence, I accepted that incorrect belief about feelings, and that misconception became part of the belief system of my ego-self. Over the past years I have come to realize that my feelings and emotions are as essential to living life as a compass and charts are to a sailor on the high seas. Without an awareness of my emotions and feelings, I am unaware of where I am, where I am going now, and where I want to go in the future.

As I said earlier, true feelings are the language of the heart, the natural Self, wisdom. As we navigate through life, we must give reverence and awareness to our feelings: they tell us when we are moving out of alignment with our spiritual Self and into the belief system of our ego-self. If we are operating from an unhealthy habit like denial, we will experience progressively growing feelings of discomfort. For example, if I am asked to do something, like write an article for a magazine or go out for a social event, my true feelings will tell me what I should do—if I listen deeply to them. My ego-self, which was trained to "be polite," "think of others, not yourself," and "don't offend anyone," will make me feel compelled to say "yes," even though I may feel in my heart that the timing isn't right or it isn't a good fit for me. If I notice that I am experiencing guilt or an uncomfortable compulsion to say "yes," that is information. What was once hidden from my conscious mind now has light on it. Once an old pattern is revealed for what it is, we are no longer controlled by that pattern of thinking.

I now see my discomfort as a moving away from the balance of my natural Self. Because I respect that feeling, I will take the time needed to reflect on this wisdom that is coming from my natural Self. At other times I will say "yes" to the earlier examples and it will feel just great, so there is no signal alerting me to listen deeper and reflect. That too is information.

Denying feelings and emotions is like ignoring a clinking in the engine of our car. If we "fix it" by putting soundproof insulation under the hood, the clinking doesn't go away; we just can't hear it. If we ignore it or camouflage it long enough, we end up with serious problems—a broken engine, or a broken marriage.

Although it is possible to turn a deaf ear to our feelings, it becomes more difficult to do so over time. The sensations we experience when we move away from balance may become more intense as we continue to ignore our inner guidance system, and the stress from living in our separated self may manifest as physical illness. Fortunately, our feelings will never give up trying to get our attention. No matter how much we deny, rationalize, or project onto others, the truth of the natural Self remains—it is our true heritage. The more we realize this, the more we will respect our feelings, the easier our lives will become, and the more loving our relationships will be.

PROJECTION When we project our unwanted negative emotions outside ourselves, we blame others and the world for our experiences. We may blame accidents or acts of nature that seem to interrupt our plans. We may blame lack of money or our wife, husband, or partner for our unhappiness. The common thread is that we don't take responsibility. We don't see that we are responsible for our thinking and it is our thinking that creates our experience, no matter what is coming our way.

Before I realized these principles, my life was like a rudderless ship, blown about by the changing winds of circumstances and other people. I felt like a victim of others, my past, and the events of life. I was constantly analyzing my emotions, replaying the "causes" in my head, and trying to figure out why I was feeling what I was feeling, who was to blame, and what I could do to change things. Instead of listening to my true feelings, I was caught in projection and "analysis paralysis." I didn't know that true feelings are information from the natural Self that simply asks for our awareness—they require no analysis, interpretation, figuring out, or any other intellectual exercise.

When we are caught up in the habit of projection, we are responding to a stimulus from our belief system rather than our true feeling or natural Self. We have an emotional reaction, usually in reaction to some external event—the slow traffic, an annoying habit of our partner, an unmet expectation, and so on. These events look to us like the causes of our emotions, rather than neutral occurrences. But if outside circumstances were truly the cause of our emotions, then all people experiencing the same outside event would have the exact emotional reaction. And that just isn't the case.

The truth is that each of us responds differently, according to our separate realities. And, as we learned in the previous chapter, we create our separate realities from our use of the powers of Mind, Thought, and Consciousness. Invisibly, we use these three powers to create our experience—every emotion, sensation, perception, and reaction. Thus, our true feelings and emotions are gifts—the navigational instruments we use to tell us whether we are experiencing the natural Self or experiencing the projections of the separated thought system. My student Janet's story illustrates this concept in her own words.

## Janet's Story

୨୦୨

Making assumptions was one of the worst problems John and I had before we gained an understanding of Health Realization. When the kids were younger, the house would often be less than perfect. If John made a comment like, "Boy, the kitchen floor really needs cleaning," I would go through the roof. That was a clue to me that he thought I was a crappy housekeeper.

"You think I'm a terrible housekeeper?" I'd say. "What the hell do you expect me to do? I work forty hours a week, I balance the checkbook, pay the bills. What do you expect?" I would immediately assume that John's statement about the floor was a judgment about my ability to keep house, rather than just an observation about the state of the kitchen floor. He actually shared the housework fifty-fifty, but I guess I just had it instilled in my head that it is the woman's job to do the housework and her worth is judged on the house she keeps. It was an old tape.

Another one that really got to me was that whenever I would go for a short drive, like to the store, John would always say, "Be careful." And I'd say, "Does he think I'm an idiot? Does he think I don't know how to drive a car, like I'm totally incompetent?!"

One day, my daughter interrupted my rant and said, "Gee Mom, I think it's sweet that he says that to you."

"What?" I said, completely puzzled.

"Why do you think he says that to you?"

"Oh," I said. "I never thought about it that way. That *is* really sweet." It hit me that for years I had resented his insinuations that I was a bad driver, only to realize later that he was expressing caring.

Once I realized it was my assumptions, not his words, that were creating my emotional reaction, I was free to accept the true meaning of what John was saying.

Janet saw the negative result of her projected thinking. She saw how her own interpretations and assumptions of what John intended had distorted her perception of their relationship. This insight has led her and John to a transformed relationship—from one of constant fighting and bickering to one of humor, love, and gratitude.

When we assume, expect, or anticipate, we are projecting our own thoughts from our ego-self onto the situation. We shadowbox with our ego, thinking it is the other person that we are fighting. All human beings, including myself, innocently do this when we are operating from our ego. However, once we listen deeply, we can begin to get a sense of whether our experience is coming from a projection—the sediment in the river that blocks clear thinking—or from the truth—flowing clear water.

Any time we deny or project, we stop the flow of our natural feelings and the wisdom they provide. We create a state of separation from the natural Self. In this state we may feel disconnected from ourselves or from our wife, husband, or partner. In short, we block our spiritual connection with Mind—the source of all things.

## Love: The Response of the Natural Self

When we respond from the natural Self, we experience wholeness and timeless love. When we listen deeply to our true feelings, we are guided to experience life as it was intended. In this state of wholehearted awareness, our feelings naturally flow. We do not experience separation or create blocks by denying or projecting. Instead, we transform existing blocks into awareness as well. Our true feelings come to us as wisdom, intuition, and insights—they show us how to make known or reveal what was invisible or unknown to us before.

For example, if we have an insight that comes from our natural Self that it is time to create more intimacy or solve a particular problem in our relationship, and we trust the intelligence of our true feelings, then we remain connected to the Universal Mind. That connection brings awareness and knowing to all situations. When we respond from love, we see the truth of the situation. Through our loving response we create a new reality. Whatever reality we create from our true Self, timeless love, will be in alignment with the true Self of our partner. On the level of timeless love we are all the same. This level is where intimacy lives and problems do not exist. At this heart-to-heart level, we are all in union—what is acceptable and harmonious for one is compatible and harmonious for another.

How do we return to this state of wholeness? By accepting ourselves as we are—with all of our feelings and our emotional responses to those feelings. Through acceptance, the feelings and emotions we denied and projected in fear we can now embrace in love, without judgment, and allow those feelings to flow. Once we accept our denied feelings and projected emotions and return them to the natural Self, they are transformed and reintegrated as Universal Love. This is the power of acceptance. This is the power of slowing down to the speed of love.

## Misunderstanding the Voice of Our True Feelings

Sometimes we misinterpret the feeling's message. If we don't quiet down and listen to what our true feelings are telling us, we may be left with what appears to be a vague, uneasy feeling. The feeling may not be vague at the onset, but as we innocently try to silence it with rationalization, we obscure the message and are left feeling uneasy. Instead of letting our wisdom surface, we may begin to turn on the intellectual computer. I am not saying that the intellect is the bad guy. When it is used in conjunction with the natural Self, we are acting wholeheartedly. However, if we are operating from the ego-self, then we use our intellect in an inappropriate manner. When we use our intellect to try and "figure out" our deeper feelings (intuition, hunches, gut feelings, murmurs of the heart), we miss out on our greatest asset. We can also damage the delicate sprout of a feeling that is just emerging, by making intellectual interpretations of it.

## Listen to the Children

I heard a story while giving a Health Realization seminar in Switzerland that is a perfect illustration of how we can misinterpret the voice of our true feelings.

On the first day of the seminar, I requested that the participants notice their thoughts after they left the seminar for the day—not judge them or do anything with them, but just observe them and let them flow. On the next day, I asked people to report on what they had noticed about their thinking.

One woman said, "Oh, I was so surprised by how negative my thinking was." She then related her experience of the night before, when she went on a school outing with her grandchildren.

"It was to be a very special night," she said, "a traditional walk in the woods at night in Switzerland to celebrate the 'journey of lights.' The grandchildren were so excited! Thei  schoolteacher was leading the excursion. The normal route for this annual event had been hit by a storm, and there were many trees crossing over the trail. The walk was through the Swiss mountains on steep trails covered with fallen trees, and it was pitch dark except for their flashlights. The children kept saying, 'Grandmama, shouldn't we turn back? It seems very dangerous.' I felt in my heart that they were right, but I thought that I should trust the teacher.

"I said to my grandchildren, 'No, it will be all right. Just be careful.'

"But the children persisted and one said, 'Grandmama, our teacher is wrong, this is really dangerous. Someone could get hurt!'

"I am also a teacher, but still I felt that I should respect my grandchildren's teacher and not go against her authority. I rationalized that the teacher must be competent; she had done this before, and so on. But my grandchildren's fears kept haunting me. Somehow I knew they were right, but I talked myself out of it because I didn't want to be negative.

"The next day, my grandson told me of a dream he had about the walk, and in it he realized that it was really dangerous and they shouldn't have done it. I knew he was right.

"I was so apprehensive, and my thoughts were so negative when I was on that walk, that I couldn't quit thinking, 'Why is she taking us on this path? It's too dangerous.'

"I really tried hard to think positive," she said.

"Although, as we walked higher," she continued, hoping to show the optimistic aspects of the trip, "the view was beautiful—a dancing string of light from our flashlights surrounded the lake and connected us. Oh, I thought, this is what she wants us to experience. Even though I could see how beautiful it was and that the teacher did have a purpose for taking us on this particular trail, I kept being drawn back to my uncomfortable feeling about the risk and that it was too slippery for young children. I really tried to be positive," she repeated.

As the woman talked, I listened deeply, beyond what she was saying. And then I asked, "Why do you see your thinking as negative?"

She explained that she was uncomfortable, so it must have been negative. I surprised her by saying that she was not being negative, that her feeling was her wisdom telling her that the circumstances were not safe and that was why she had a feeling of discomfort. The situation was not in alignment with the common sense of her natural Self. It was a great teaching opportunity for me to illustrate how easily we talk ourselves out of our common sense. It also illustrated how wise young children can be and that we should listen to them. They are not yet as contaminated with opinions and beliefs as we are. In hindsight, I'm sure the grandmother would have trusted her feelings and those of her grandchildren and possibly decided to take them home early.

I have described just a few of the most common ways we block our awareness of the feelings of the natural Self. So how do we know if our sensations are our true feelings or our emotions and how do we know which source they are coming from—the natural Self or the ego-self?

## Listening for the Grain of Truth

Listening to our true Self is a little like trying to approach a wild animal in the forest. You must be very still and respect its domain. Don't rush to it in impatience. Let it come to you. Aggressiveness, impatience, and force all repel the wild animal, and so too, our inner feelings. Unlike the wild animal, however, these feelings are with us always, guiding us each step of the way in our relationships and through all of life, closer than a heartbeat. "Listen, like an explorer in the wilderness," as my wife Michael so beautifully illustrates in this poem about the voice of our spiritual Self—to our inner feelings:

### Closer Than a Heartbeat

*I speak not the language of the intellect, that isn't my way.*
*I travel the pathways of your nerves and enliven your senses.*
*I construct the fibers of your dreams and walk the corridors of*
 *your mind.*

*I am communication at the subtlest level—*
*My thoughts are your true desires.*
*I am in every corner of your experience . . . expressing and guiding.*

*Hear me and I will ease your pain,*
*Respect me and I will show you the way.*
*Love me and you will love yourself and all the world around you.*

*Listen, I am the whisper in your feeling—my words are ever-present.*
*Listen—learn the language of the experience—*
*You have known it from birth.*

*Listen, like an explorer in the wilderness,*
*Guided by the signals of nature—a turned leaf, a subtle yearning—*
*My voice will become louder when magnified by your awareness.*

*I speak through the body and well in emotion.*
*I penetrate your dreams and*
*Fuel your desires.*

*I am the essence,*
*The driving force of your existence—*
*Body, mind, spirit are all aspects of the whole.*

*My language is simplicity*
*Beyond intellectual translations that judge, complicate, and define.*
*I flow, I transform . . . I am before time.*

*Catch me in the moment,*
*I have all the answers—*
*I cannot be saved for the future or confined in the brain.*

*My environment is the moment—it is there that I thrive.*
*Do not worry, I am in every moment, available at all times . . .*
*Closer than a heartbeat.*

*—Michael Bailey*

Awareness is the first guideline for listening to our feelings. As we have spoken of earlier in this chapter and as the poem illustrates, our physical bodies reflect the quality and source of our thinking through sensations, emotions, and feelings of comfort (balance) and discomfort (imbalance). These feelings and sensations are our friends. They are a language spoken through our breathing, our heart rate, our muscle tension, and all other physical sensations. It is often through discomfort that our awareness is aroused. Once the feelings have our attention, it is what we do with that awareness that determines whether we will help or hurt our relationship and ourselves.

Acceptance of our feelings and emotions is the next guideline for listening to our inner feelings. Acceptance disengages our ego and allows us to hear the messages of the heart. This doesn't mean that we immediately act on all that we feel, merely that we move into a state of acceptance. From that state, we can access the natural stillness of our mind and heart in union. Awareness and acceptance take us to the point of discernment. In a calm mind we access our wisdom and time-less love.

The last guideline is expression. Sometimes our feelings only need our awareness and acceptance to reveal their guidance. Other times, we are guided from within to express in unity with others our heart-felt dreams and desires. When we speak from our hearts, we are in union with our natural Self. When another deeply listens to us while we are speaking from the heart, we exist in unity and feel a deep sense of connection—the true form of intimacy.

In the next chapter, we will further explore what speaking from the heart is, how to have a heart-to-heart talk, and the basis of effective communication.

# 7

# SPEAK FROM THE HEART

{← ∘ — ∘ →}

THE NIGHT IN THE Bad Habit Cafe when Michael told me that, in her experience, I was not a good listener, is a great example of speaking from the heart. She spoke with love, absolute honesty, with no regard for the possible consequences of her speaking. She just knew she had to speak to me from her true Self. At that time in our relationship's history, our level of awareness of how to have a true heart-to-heart was not very developed. Consequently, her inner voice of truth kept getting louder and louder, until she could contain it no more. As I listened, I seemed to have no choice but to give her words reverence and respect—because speaking from the heart commands attention and respect. When people speak "their truth," they connect with the truth in everyone.

Listening deeply and speaking from the heart are intimately connected. You cannot speak from the heart until you listen deeply to the feelings of your natural Self. As you realize how to speak your truth, you will apply all you discovered in the two earlier chapters on deep listening and listening to your feelings. Deep listening is more than listening to others; it is being conscious of your own feelings, instincts, intuitions, and gut reactions. This is listening within.

What is within is not always altogether clear to us until we share it with others. This phenomenon is precisely what relationships are all about: sharing from our spiritual nature. When we share our natural Selves, we become connected—intimate. Speaking from the heart is sharing who we are, which is distinctly different from sharing our belief system or the persona we unknowingly make up and project. In this chapter, I will explore the realm of the heart, what it means to speak from the heart, and how to have a heart-to-heart with others.

## Wholeheartedness: Mind and Heart in Union

Children live in a world of feelings. They express them freely, act on them, and are very aware of them. As adults, we are always feeling something every moment of every day. Sometimes we are conscious of what we are feeling, other times we are not. As we go through life, some of us are taught that certain responses, such as anger, sexuality, and tenderness (if you are a male), are unacceptable. As we learn to block certain feelings, we construct a dam that stops our awareness and expression of our true feelings. We start the process of moving away from our heart and into our belief system. We begin to live our lives not from the wisdom of our true feelings, but from rules, beliefs, opinions, and injunctions. This is how we have unknowingly created the separation or split between heart and mind.

When we do not have a balance of heart and mind, our intellect can lead us astray. The intellect serves the level of consciousness that is in place in the moment. If the ego is running the show, then the intellect will support it. If the natural Self is engaged, then the intellect will support it. When the intellect is in alignment with the natural Self, the mind and heart are in balance, and we are then truly wholehearted.

The heart is our access to timeless love, and our true feelings are the messengers of the heart. Complete within our heart is the remembrance of who we are. Our natural ability to recognize the truth lies within us—whole and uncontaminated. To return to our birthright of well-being and resiliency, we must return to wholeheartedness. This begins with listening to the heart.

## Acceptance: The Power That Facilitates Change

When we remain wholehearted, we are able to observe our feelings without judgment. As we discussed earlier, in an atmosphere of acceptance, feelings emerge and become clear. Accept yourself as you are, not as who you want to be. Acceptance is the power that implements change. It doesn't mean that we accept what we don't like, whether it is a situation, a habit, a reaction, or an insecurity. It means that we simply accept that we don't like it and that we are experiencing it. Acceptance is the only way to prevent judgment. I will emphasize the power of acceptance throughout the book. Understanding this profound point will change your experience of life immeasurably.

Generally speaking, when we have a problem honoring our true feelings and trusting their wisdom, we project distrust onto others. We tend to not listen deeply, discount our partner's truth, and not give credit or trust the source of their wisdom. When we judge our true feelings or those of another, we stifle expression and thus the clarity that comes with them. This is the greatest cause of problems in relationships. Although we may give our partner permission to express his or her feelings openly, we may not be open to truly receiving them. This double message is confusing.

For example, you or your partner may be uncomfortable with certain topics, feelings, or issues. These topics or feelings may be sources of discomfort or blind spots. When these areas are brought up, you may feel like an invisible shield that you can't penetrate has just gone up. You or your partner may not even be consciously aware of these "off-limits" areas of discussion. But when the invisible shield is up, it stops the flow of a heart-to-heart conversation. One or both of you may not be willing to talk about money, sex, a past event, or anger. If you and your partner become aware of this blockage, you may or may not be able to let it go and return to a state of receptivity.

To move forward in our relationships, we need to receive each other fully. If we don't, that off-limits area will present an unhealthy climate for the whole relationship. It will become the dam in the river of flowing thoughts and feelings. To remove any barrier to heart-to-heart communication, we must be aware of the barrier or uncomfortable topic, accept ourselves and the other person, and be willing to trust our true feelings.

## Receptive Listening: Encouraging Others to Speak from the Heart

When you join in a heart-to-heart with your partner, you truly receive and experience what he or she is saying. The unity in this state allows you to transcend the limitations of language and feel what your partner's heart is saying. True thoughts that arise from unity are different from the thoughts you experience in separation. If you receive your partner fully, you will be capable of responding to him or her fully, in the present moment. Here's a story that will illustrate the power of receptivity.

## The Invisible Shield

ιΟΟι

Hal's a physician, and if you asked his patients, they would say that he is a sensitive man and a good listener. When I first met Hal, it was obvious that he was capable of relating to people on a deep level, but at times an invisible fortress protected him. It was confusing, considering his talent to deeply connect in certain situations, but like many in the helping professions, Hal didn't know much about receiving for himself.

He met Lara, and, although he was divorced and had other relationships before, he fell deeply in love for the first time. This time he was truly himself, and as a result his invisible fortress was beginning to crumble. But on occasion, Lara would remind him that his fortress was still partially intact.

Lara was aware and intuitive. She was very clear and could feel immediately when he moved out of the feeling space of his natural Self and into his ego-based thought system. Lara knew when Hal was not receiving her or another person, and she would point out these instances to him. At times, Lara would share stories from her work and Hal, being a solution-oriented guy, couldn't resist offering advice. Even though Lara had been very clear that she wanted him to just listen, he never heard her and didn't realize that he was crossing her boundaries without an invitation. He knew she was right, but because he had little experience of receiving, it was difficult for him to recognize the feeling. He trusted Lara and her intuition but didn't know what to look for.

Hal presented me with his dilemma. I knew this was a hard area for him, because two months earlier he had asked me, as a friend, to talk to him about a problem. Although he thought he was listening, he was not taking in what I had to offer. The example was fresh in my mind, so I knew what Lara was trying to show him.

"You're not receiving Lara," I told him. "It would be helpful if you got a sense of what it feels like to receive and what it feels like when you are not being received. It is like the game of hot and cold we played as children. One of the kids would yell, 'Hot . . . hotter . . . ouch, you're burning up,' as you were coming closer to the hidden object, or 'Cold . . . colder . . . ice cold,' when you were moving away from the object. Lara is a great feedback system for you. She's a great partner for the game of hot and cold."

I shared with Hal how it felt to me when he had asked me to speak to him two months earlier. I said, "It felt like you invited me to dinner and when I got to your house, the door was locked." I told him at first I didn't realize that I wasn't being fully received, but I noticed the conversation felt effortful and I found myself explaining what I meant in many ways. This was a clue—I could see that something was off. I then moved on, because I knew I wasn't being received and we weren't going anywhere productive. It seemed like a good time to go for lunch.

After lunch, something changed—the topic resurfaced, he was receptive, and I spontaneously said in two sentences what I was unable to say earlier.

When I related this past experience to Hal, he remembered that he was in a more open and willing state after lunch than before. With that awareness, Hal started to get a glimpse that being more open was linked to his willingness to let go of his illusionary protective shield. Because he was more his true Self at times with Lara he had the experience of how wonderful it is to be who we truly are.

Hal is starting to experience the feelings of true openness that are natural to his spiritual Self. He is seeing the power of willingness to fully give and receive timeless love.

Receptive listening is powerful for both the speaker and the listener because giving and receiving are one and the same thing, which I will go into more detail about in Chapter 9. Hal and the other people in this book are starting to create new relationships through their understanding of the principles of Mind, Thought, and Consciousness.

## Acceptance of the Present

The power to create a new reality comes from our oneness with Mind—the source of all things, which is at the core of true heart-to-heart communication. We won't always sustain this level of awareness and experience the feelings of our true nature, timeless love. We will move in and out of our awareness of the natural Self, but our willingness to return to the feeling is all that is necessary. Many things in our lives will take time to change, but once we begin to accept the present more frequently, we will notice phenomenal changes that are immediate.

One aspect of acceptance of the present is that we can share with our partner without limits, and we are in union with each other. At times, limitations and insecurities may surface. By merely remaining neutral and observing them without jumping to defend, blame, deny, or push them out of our awareness, we will see them dissolve. The neutral space we create with our partner is the healthy, safe environment needed to bring to light any belief that is obstructing our awareness of who we are. At times it may seem difficult and challenging, but willingness is all that is needed to let go of our beliefs and insecurities.

Could it be that simple? Yes, although sometimes you may not be willing. If that happens, trust in your true nature to reveal to you what fears you may have. You will discover beliefs that keep you from being willing to let go and experience who you truly are. Sometimes, more often in the beginning of understanding the principles, your mind and heart may conflict with old patterns of thought. The more you choose wholeheartedness as a way of life, the more this natural expression will become your norm. It will become how you relate in your relationships and how you express who you are. Old patterns will naturally drop off as you create a new life from wholeness.

Being aware of how you feel in the present moment is the path to certainty that you, like all of us, have long searched for. When you are comfortable in accepting who you are and what you feel, whatever response is appropriate for that moment will be apparent. When you trust your true feelings, you trust yourself. When you see your unity with Mind, your true identity is no longer a mystery, and trust is not a question.

## The Fear of Silence

In our speed-bound world of business and society, we seldom take time for stillness, an important aspect of listening deeply to ourselves as well as to others. We can't really be ourselves if we don't listen to our hearts. If we never experience silence, we are completely controlled by our past conditioning, other people, and the world around us. Distraction is a defense we have constructed to avoid awareness of what we are feeling. As long as we are unaware of our true feelings, we will have no self-correcting mechanism for our lives, our relationships, our health, and our environment.

I recently conducted a retreat for physicians and other health care professionals. One of the exercises we did with them was to have them reflect on the roots of their vocation, what inspired them to go into their profession, and what was in the way of following their heart now.

I also read my wife Michael's poem from the last chapter, "Closer Than a Heartbeat." When we returned to the large group and shared our reflections, many were deeply moved and felt a renewed sense of passion for their work and their relationships. Interestingly, several participants were upset by this exercise. One said, "I found this deeply disturbing. I don't know if I like what I heard from my inner Self. If I listen to what I heard, I may need to make some changes."

Three months later in the next retreat, that same physician reported that the wisdom of his natural Self was telling him that his life was totally out of balance at work and at home. At first he felt resistant to this insight; his physician belief system rationalized that it was just part of the job, but the insight persisted. A little willingness was all that was needed on his part and he began to entertain his dream to cut down to 75 percent time. Then insights occurred as to how to achieve his heartfelt desire, and he saw ways to delegate more responsibilities, which before had not seemed to be an option. He now looks ten years younger and totally happy with himself; he remarked, "I didn't realize that it was only my limited thinking that was stopping me from following my heart."

It is no wonder that so much of humanity is in the fast lane, running from the awareness of these often troubling feelings. If they only knew that their feelings were truly on their side, they would take the time to listen to them.

Listening to ourselves can be very disturbing when we judge our true feelings or when we analyze the implications of what would happen if we acted on those feelings. Trusting in the unknown is not something the ego-self is very fond of doing. The ego creates the false belief that it can predict the future and that if we listen to it (the ego), we will be in control. The truth is that the ego does not know the future; there is always an unknown quality to life.

## The Power of Trusting the Unknown

The power of creation exists in the present moment, not in the future. Endless possibilities are available in the present moment. That is why the future is unknown.

We are creative beings; we create from the unknown. The act of wondering is creative. Have you ever wondered, "How does that work?" or "What does that mean?" Have you ever let the thought go and later on that day or on another day, you have an insight or you notice something—and there's your answer from out of the blue? This example of trusting in your creative intelligence is what it is like to make the unknown known through discovery. You may have wondered, "What is love, really?" or "How do relationships work?" or "How can I have a happy relationship?" In asking such questions, you have brought your awareness to the subject. Awareness is powerful, especially when you're conscious of your true nature.

We are designed to discover through reflection. That doesn't mean we wouldn't read a book or talk to someone to get information; it means that we know we are guided from the inside out. We can recognize the truth when we hear it, because the truth is already written in our hearts, and when we hear or read it we are remembering it from the depth of our spirit.

Not knowing is not bad, it just is. It is actually very freeing and honest to accept that we don't know the future or an answer to a question. Acceptance of not knowing is what takes us into *discovery*, which is a state of being that reveals the truth to us in each moment through our inner intelligence. We are brought to more awareness by curiosity and a willingness to make known what is unknown. Slowing down to the speed of love is remaining in a constant state of coming to know—it is an ongoing state of discovery.

## 🞉 NOT KNOWING AND LOVING IT

For the next week, try the same exercise that I give to my students. For any issue—relationship-related or not—just give yourself permission to not know the answer. Answer the question with another question. Your questions will usually get deeper and go to the root of the issue.

For example, in my training program called "Teaching from the Heart," I give my students an exercise to do for a whole month. For the next month, with any issue or problem, I instruct them to not try to answer their questions. Instead, I ask them to answer the question with another question, or say, "I don't know." They are asked to do this until we return together next month. Even though this exercise is initially very awkward, the response is always very positive. Students share that they had more insights and creative thinking than they ever had before, they feel a huge reduction in worry and stress, and they are relieved to not have to be in control and have the answer. This is how we discover the truth—by being comfortable with the unknown and by removing from the process the ego-based pressure of having to know.

### Intellectualizing Our Feelings

We also block awareness through intellectualizing our true feelings. We must do nothing more than listen quietly to our feelings. Simple awareness is all that is necessary to reveal the heart. As I explained in Chapter 6, anything more than awareness takes us back into our intel-

**∞ LET YOUR HEART SPEAK**

As a practice, take a moment now to write down your feelings on a piece of paper, without judging what you write. Don't censor, judge, analyze, or hold back in any way. Just let your heart speak to you. After you are finished, let the feelings just be there—don't try to do anything with them or figure out what they mean. Ask yourself questions and just see what comes.

lect—and leads to judging, analyzing, comparing, labeling, doubting, second-guessing, or processing—all of which muddy up the water again. It is so simple to listen to your heart. It is awareness without interpretation.

Many people today keep journals. They enjoy that they are able to express their deepest feelings and thoughts without fear of judgment. They often discover things they didn't know they were feeling, dreaming of, or intuiting about their lives. Speaking from the heart is much like journaling—only doing it with another person.

## Speaking from the Heart

When you listen within to your heart, you will often hear the unexpected—an area of your life that needs to change, an obstacle that you have been denying in your relationship, a physical or emotional imbalance.

Once you are aware of the voice of your heart, the next step, as mentioned before, is acceptance. We often mistakenly go to work on figuring out or fixing the imbalances, once we have become aware that they are in our lives. It's best to begin by simply accepting what you are feeling; don't judge, analyze, or rush to come up with an answer. Once you are aware of and have accepted your feeling, the next step is to express it. Expressing is speaking from the heart. In summary, the process is awareness, acceptance, and expression.

Let me give you a personal example that involved a time in my life when I was getting a strong feeling that the direction of my career needed to change. I had been a psychotherapist for twenty-five years. I loved counseling people, and I couldn't imagine not doing this type of work. And it was my main source of income. Nonetheless, I kept having this gnawing feeling that it was time to move on. Little aspects of the job were starting to not be enjoyable, and I wanted more time to write and devote myself to teaching and doing seminars. The counseling kept me from being mobile and free to travel. Yet, whenever I would consider the possibility of not doing counseling, I would feel insecure about the finances and my identity.

My wife and I decided to take a week at our cabin and do nothing but relax and make time for reflection. We decided to help each other in our career directions by asking open questions and just listening deeply to each other without processing the details or trying to come up with answers. As the week went on, my feelings about my career got much clearer. I knew what I needed to do. I felt a depth of certainty even though the insecure thoughts periodically came to mind. I shared my dreams and aspirations with Michael many times, and with each time of sharing from my heart, I became clearer and more certain of my direction. She listened deeply and didn't judge or try to answer questions for me, which helped me get clearer by making the space to hear my own true feelings.

When I returned home, I put into motion the decision I had realized at the cabin. All my fears were, of course, unfounded, and I have never regretted the decision. Within a short time I had enough new consulting business to make up for the loss in counseling business. I did better that year financially than I ever had before. Most important, I had followed my heart's desire that led my vocation in an inspired new direction.

Sharing with your partner, both of you anchored in union with Universal Mind, is a powerful experience. Each of you speaks from the state of discovery that reflects the wisdom of your natural Self, in unity. Your partner in this heart-to-heart sharing is not giving you beliefs and opinions, but sharing his or her wisdom and pointing you back to yours.

There are many reasons to share from the heart, one of which is to become clear about personal decisions, as in the previous example. However, many other benefits come from sharing from the heart: personal transformation, conflict resolution, and addressing impasses in relationships and misunderstandings. Sometimes conflicts, impasses, and misunderstandings are more intimidating because they involve sep-

## ∞ Guidelines for a Heart-to-Heart

To ease the way for a true heart-to-heart interaction, we need to follow several guidelines. These are not rules or techniques, but commonsense elements to any productive interaction. They are:

- Listen deeply to your own wisdom and that of your partner.
- Let go of any investment in the outcome of the sharing.
- Keep your bearings and monitor the tone.
- Ask permission.
- Share and receive from the heart (unrehearsed, spontaneous).
- Maintain rapport and respect.

arate perceptions of a situation, strong emotions, and habitual patterns of resolving problems between people in a relationship.

## Let Go of Investment in the Outcome

Because we have already spoken of listening deeply to our own wisdom, which is the first guideline for a heart-to-heart talk, I would like to explore the second guideline: let go of any investment you may have in the outcome.

We may experience fear for many reasons. It may alert us to remove ourself from a situation or tell us to let go of our negative thoughts. Regardless, fear is always a signal to listen deeply to our true Self. Fear that results from our investment in the outcome may occur when issues are important to us. For example, if we are invested in buying a particular house or going to a particular location for a vacation, we may be afraid we won't get our way. Fear of not getting your way is the opposite of trust. Fear can lead to controlling thoughts and aggressiveness. This is why when we are invested in the outcome, we get so anxious and why we're often angry when things aren't going our way. Nevertheless, it is imperative that we leave our egos at the door when speaking from the heart; it is the only way to access our true Self. The ego's thinking is rigid and narrow. The natural Self's thinking is wise and open, and will automatically guide us to a harmonious outcome. When we trust the natural Self, we aren't invested in a specific outcome, but instead we are open to an expanse of creative possibilities. We can accept that we are having fearful thoughts and sensations and allow our minds to quiet down so that we may receive an insight from within.

Another reason for this guideline is that if we are invested in the outcome, the other person will always sense this and usually will respond defensively and with resistance.

## Keep Your Bearings and Monitor the Tone

You cannot truly speak from the heart when you have lost your bearings or the tone is off. Keeping your bearings means speaking from the natural Self, not the ego-self. Your feelings and emotions will let you know if you have kept your bearings and are in a place of timeless love, or if you have lost them and are in a place of fear. A fearful emotion means that you have lost awareness of the balance of your true Self. Timeless love means that you are grounded in the awareness of your natural Self. An emotional reaction may take the form of investment, impatience, judgment, hopelessness, confusion, anger, or blame. Love, on the other hand, is patient, strong, firm, clear, compassionate, calm, and accepting. Listen to your feelings and emotions as a guidance system for your state of mind. When you have lost your bearings, all you need to do is back off and just listen more deeply.

The tone is the quality of the interaction between the two of you. It is the quality of rapport, trust, openness, and deep listening. If you are in a state of observance, you can tell when the tone has gone bad. For example, when I am teaching a couple how to have a heart-to-heart, I will often have them practice in my presence. They will sometimes get so involved in the content of the discussion that they forget to observe the tone or their bearings. I will interrupt them and point out whenever they have lost the awareness of the tone. Eventually, they start to feel it themselves. Awareness of the tone requires a slight noticing every so often, kind of like checking your rearview mirror. It doesn't take away from the heart-to-heart; it just alerts you to danger before it overcomes you.

As you become more aware of your true feelings, you may become aware of particular patterns of thinking that take you away from loving, balanced feelings and create an interruption in the tone. For example, in my experience, I have noticed that when I focus a lot of energy on a past event, it is impossible for me to bring that event up to illustrate a point without losing my perspective and becoming lost in the details. I see that until I have understanding and perspective on the past, it is necessary for me to find a neutral way to explain myself. This awareness of my personal pitfalls helps me keep my bearings in a heart-to-heart exchange.

## Ask Permission

People who know each other well often skip this step. They assume they have permission to have a heart-to-heart, because they are married, for example, or because they are the parent. *Never assume permission.* Always ask for it before you go into the realm of the heart—it is sacred ground. Asking permission can be as simple as "Can we have a talk?" to "I have something very important to talk with you about. When would be a good time for you, and are you willing to hear me out?" Even during a heartfelt exchange, it is important to reestablish permission periodically, especially if you notice the other person is getting defensive or is not listening. "Is it still OK to talk to you about this?" Getting and keeping permission goes a long way to keeping the listening deep and the mind open.

We all know of relationships where one person's asking to have a talk and the other person reacts by rolling his or her eyes and saying something like, "This again?" We each bring our misunderstandings and insecure habits into our relationships. From these habits we create unhealthy dynamics. Some of us blame and complain to be heard, others may talk *at* their partner rather than *to* them, while another may just tune everything out in self-defense. Whatever pattern we have innocently created with each other is a barrier to sharing our natural Self. Fortunately, when we come from the secure grounding of timeless love it changes the dynamic.

It is important to be grounded in the first three guidelines when you ask permission, otherwise you will get resistance and wonder why. Listen to your wisdom; is it an appropriate time to ask for a heart-to-heart talk? Let go of any investment; are you invested in changing your partner or are you looking for a deeper spiritual awareness for yourself? Keep your bearings and monitor the tone; are you asking permission from a loving feeling? If your partner is open, and you are in alignment with these guidelines, the effect will be positive.

Many people resist having a talk because they are afraid that they will be blamed or judged. Asking to speak from your heart to gain peace for yourself is very different from trying to "fix" your partner and getting him or her to change. As we have discussed throughout the book, look within yourself for changes, not to your partner. Even in heart-to-heart communication it's not about the other person. It is about each of us coming together to express, as best as we can, what is in our heart and is true for us.

When Michael spoke to me in the Bad Habit Cafe about listening, she did not blame or try to change me; she spoke from her heart. She knew that I was unaware of my bad listening habits and how adversely it was affecting our relationship. In short, she saw my innocence. She told me what was true for her, what would be nurturing for her, and how it feels to be truly listened to. She did not judge me or tell me that I had to do anything. She hoped I would take what she said to heart, but she knew that was up to me. Michael spoke from her heart because she was listening to her inner feelings. She did it for her own spiritual awareness, which is all anyone can do. What the other person does in response is his or her own free choice.

Even if your partner's habit is to resist communication, it will be a different dynamic if you remain in the feeling of timeless love. You will not be affected the same way you may have been in the past; your common sense will come to your aid. It takes time to break old habits and we all have our blind spots. Extending timeless love to your partner is very powerful. Every one of us is timeless love inside, and we each have the ability to access it, although some may choose to hang on to the fear and insecurity of their ego belief system. If your partner continually refuses to have a heart-to-heart, you will see what to do in light of the circumstances. Some, but few, block themselves off from even the most loving intentions.

## Share and Receive from the Heart

Sharing from the heart requires no rehearsing, agenda, or plan. In fact, all of those will get in the way of having a heart-to-heart. Trust your true feelings and thoughts that come from the heart. They know where they are going, even if you don't think so. The wisdom of the heart is infinite and has the solutions to all problems and all misunderstandings. At the level of the heart, we are all united. We are one when we share and listen from the heart. The heart is our common ground, our undivided Self. Trust your heart—it knows.

## Maintain Rapport and Respect

It is important to maintain respect for the other person and yourself throughout the heart-to-heart. Reflect periodically to see if you are coming from a place of respect and if you have rapport with the other person. You can tell quite easily if you do and you don't have to be a psychologist to tell. Again, listen to the feelings; they will be your guides.

The following story is an example of a couple's first heart-to-heart about an extremely sensitive and emotionally charged issue.

## A Wounded Heart

ဢ

A couple I once saw was dealing with the husband's infidelity, which the wife had recently found out about. He had had a one-night encounter, a year before, with a woman he met while he was out of town on business. Cheating on his wife was not something he thought he would ever do. This crisis instigated their seeking marriage counseling, although they had been growing apart progressively for fifteen years.

Lydia felt that Dan didn't love her anymore, he had become distant over the years and always seemed preoccupied by his work. He didn't seem open to talking or changing and she felt unloved and resentful. Her anger and resentful emotions had reached a peak about nine months prior to the infidelity. As a result, Dan and Lydia were living parallel lives without intimacy or communication and Lydia's ever-growing resentment was pushing Dan even further away. They didn't have enough rapport nor did they know how to speak and listen from the heart to address the growing distance between them.

When they arrived at the second session, Dan was filled with shame and guilt, Lydia with hurt and anger. She wasn't sure if she could continue the marriage. He couldn't look either of us in the eye. Lydia looked so angry that I thought she would scream at any moment.

In their first session, before they disclosed to me that he had had an affair, they were very evasive. This session, Dan was dreading the exposure but Lydia felt she had no choice but to reveal the source of her pain. With the safe environment of a therapist's office and the guidance of how to have a heart-to-heart, they felt freer to express their feelings. Finally, Lydia asked his permission to tell me about "the secret." He was reluctant, but finally said "yes."

For the next fifteen minutes Lydia poured out her heart. "I feel so hurt and angry," she said. "I feel betrayed. I don't know how I can love and trust you again. I feel so responsible at times. I know that I haven't been very responsive to you, for a long time. I've been so angry and hurt; all you seem interested in is your job and not me; you haven't had time for our relationship."

Dan replied, "How do you think I feel, the way you have been treating me for the past number of months? It feels like you didn't care about me anymore, that you are tired of our marriage. You have been so hard to be around; you snap at me, you always act like you are irritated with me, and before being unfaithful I hadn't done anything." He realized the one-night stand was an expression of his frustration and thoughts of rejection.

After her husband's disclosure about the one-night stand, Lydia expressed all of the emotions she was experiencing and was able to be truthful to herself and to him. At the end of it she felt a tremendous relief. She said things she didn't know were in her, and she seemed to have no control over what came out of her mouth.

Paradoxically, she felt more connected to Dan than before. She hadn't resolved her emotions of deep hurt and anger, but this was a beginning. Lydia could see that it was more than just about Dan's infidelity. For fifteen years she and Dan had both innocently contributed to the discordant state of their relationship. This moment of speaking from her inner spirit became the catalyst for them to continue counseling and begin a process to see how to live from their spiritual nature. Dan was deeply sorry for the pain he had caused Lydia. From hearing her share her experience, he had gained some understanding of why she felt resentful and had pushed him away. He could see how his habit of throwing himself into his work had made Lydia think he was rejecting her.

Although this heart-to-heart was mostly emotional catharsis, it set the stage for many more heart-to-hearts that progressed over the next year and a half. They are still involved in this process. I will continue their story, as things are a year later, in the next chapter on forgiveness.

# Walking into the Unknown

When we have a heart-to-heart, we have no idea where it is going or where it will end up. Fear is why people avoid speaking from the heart and listening from the heart—fear that they will have no control. In fact, the ego never has control; it just operates from the illusion that it does. Trusting in the unknown is key to being able to speak our minds from our hearts. It takes the reliance off of our intellect and our ideas of life, and puts our reliance where it rightfully is—in the hands of our natural Self. No risk is really involved in having a heartfelt exchange; there just appears to be a risk from the stance of fear. Whenever I have had a true talk from my heart to another's, it has always ended in greater understanding, healing, and a deeper connection. Next, I will share another example of a heart-to-heart about being present.

### She Missed His Presence

ෆ

Will and Jean had been married for ten years. They met and fell deeply in love. After a few years they began to have children, three in a row. As Jean became more occupied with the children, Will became more absorbed in his work as a stockbroker. He was seldom at home, and when he was there, he was rarely involved with the family. He began having affairs, and Jean eventually found out.

They initially came to see me because of the crisis precipitated by Will's infidelities. However, it became clear early on that the intimacy they once shared had left long before the affairs. In their counseling, they learned the principles we have been discussing in this book, and yet they were still very stuck. Something kept getting in the way, so I taught them the five guidelines of how to have a heart-to-heart.

As Jean began to listen to herself better, she realized that she had grown accustomed to Will's distance and lack of presence. She missed him and wanted to feel as close to him as she had been when they first fell in love, but he was still very preoccupied. (This illustrates the first point of this process—listen to yourself.)

One night she decided to ask Will if they could talk. (Guideline four: ask permission.) He was committed to saving their marriage, so he agreed. She began to tell him about how he seemed distant. He was never really with her or the kids. His mind was always on work or the chores he had to do around the house.

"I really want you to be with me wholeheartedly," she pleaded, her eyes heavy with tears of sadness. "I miss you." (Guideline five: share and receive from the heart.)

He listened, as he hadn't done in years. As he saw her genuine love for him, he saw how much he had hurt her and how they had slowly but surely slipped away from each other. (Guideline one: listen deeply to your wisdom and that of your partner.) "I miss you too, sweetie," he said. "I thought you really didn't need me or want me after the kids were born. There didn't seem to be room for me in your life."

For a moment Jean became defensive. She thought, "Are you saying it's my fault you had an affair?" She could feel the anger growing. But she recognized that she was losing her bearings, and she cleared her mind until she felt grounded again. It then occurred to her that she had taken his last remark very personally and read accusations into it. As a result, she had reacted defensively and with anger. But she realized she didn't have to project that kind of meaning onto his words. (Guideline three: keep your bearings and monitor the tone.) After a moment she said, "I'm so glad you feel the way I do. Can we start again?"

They embraced and recommitted to each other to be as present as possible and to share the love between them once again. This was another turning point in their relationship, though not the last one. Change is an upward spiral, leading us to deeper understanding and levels of intimacy.

Having a heart-to-heart is like the emergency road service of relationships. When we periodically run out of gas, get into an accident, or communication breaks down, it's nice to know there is a way out of trouble. The next chapter deals with another type of heart-to-heart, often a more difficult one—a heart-to-heart involving forgiveness.

# 8

# FORGIVENESS AS A WAY OF LIFE

❦∘——∘❦

*Only forgiveness replaces judgment, but true forgiveness is as foreign to you as is true love. You think forgiveness looks upon another in judgment and pardons the wrongs you would enumerate. True forgiveness simply looks past illusion to the truth where there are no sins to be forgiven, no wrongs to be pardoned. Forgiveness looks on innocence and sees it where judgment would see it not.*

—MARI PERRON AND DANIEL ODEGARD, *A Course of Love*

FORGIVENESS IS ACCEPTANCE. When you accept someone, you forgive him or her. It does not mean you have to believe that the behavior was appropriate or fair; it just means you are accepting that it happened. It happened because in that person's separate reality, it was all he or she could see at the time. Forgiveness also means that you accept your emotions and reactions to the other person. By accepting yourself and the other person, your mind will be able to return to peace. Acceptance recognizes everyone's innocence and sees through the mask of the ego to the spiritual Self. Acceptance prevents judgment. It lets us see everything in life fresh.

Forgiveness is a prerequisite to true love. You cannot have a loving relationship where judgment, resentment, guilt (judging yourself), or blame exist. Forgiveness is the ability to see innocence in another, without judgment. Most of my life I was taught that forgiveness had two components:

1. Judge someone as wrong, evil, sinful, bad, crazy, and/or judge that person's wrong actions.
2. Then pardon or forgive that person out of the goodness of your heart, or because it is the "right" thing to do.

I always thought forgiving was a very hard thing to do. I seemed to forgive people in my head, but my emotions weren't really aligned. Later the same resentments would resurface. I believed, as a good Christian, that forgiveness was a good and noble thing to do; I just couldn't get my whole self into it. I now see that this was because I saw myself as separate from (and better than) the other person.

A certain superiority resides in false forgiveness. True forgiveness is wholehearted—mind and heart are joined in the true spirit of forgiveness. No backlash exists with this kind of forgiveness; it is complete and permanent. This chapter is about how to achieve wholehearted forgiveness, because without it, true love in any relationship is impossible.

Forgiveness is the balm that heals all relationships. When we forgive another, it frees us from the past and allows us to fully live in the present. Forgiveness can be for a particular act, transgression, event, or for a whole pattern of behavior over a period of time (such as abuse or alcoholism).

I would like you to consider a larger definition of forgiveness that broadens our concept of it to a way of life. When we value forgiveness as a way of life, we see that not forgiving (holding on to resentment or guilt) will hold us back from loving fully. Anything that holds us back from loving will block our hearts from experiencing timeless love.

What is forgiveness? It is a change in our awareness of reality—a change in our level of understanding of the past and our relationship to others. Forgiveness is a way of seeing the past, even five minutes ago, with compassion and a new way of understanding the person, the act, or the omission. Forgiveness is not merely saying the words, "I forgive you"; it is a change in our level of understanding and feeling. It is a release of all anger or guilt. Forgiveness sees past the illusion that we are totally separate beings, or that one of us is better than another, to the truth that we are all one.

True forgiveness sees that there is nothing and never was anything to forgive in the first place. That doesn't mean that the people we forgive aren't responsible for their actions, it just means that, according to their distorted ego-belief system, they believed that their behavior was valid or that they had no other choice considering the circumstances. Belief systems are very deceptive. Sometimes people can do devastating harm with the noblest of intentions. As Jesus said on the cross, "Forgive them, for they know not what they do." When we see the innocence of others and ourselves in creating our reality and experience through the power of the three principles, we understand that all of us are doing the best we can at the moment, given our level of awareness at the time. Whatever was done was done in innocence, through the illusion of being separate.

When we see the healing power of forgiveness for ourselves and for our relationships, we will more readily forgive. We will adopt forgiveness as a way of life.

## A Story of Forgiveness

For much of my childhood and young adulthood, I had a troubling relationship with my father. To me he appeared unloving, disapproving, emotionally distant, and rejecting. All of my life I desperately wanted his approval, his pride in me as a son, but I only felt his judgment and disapproval. Eventually, I grew to dislike my father, and yet I always prayed that we could connect and heal our relationship.

I spent many years in therapy talking to a therapist about my anger toward my dad. I even beat pillows, shouting my anger at him in hopes that it would heal our relationship and me. I eventually had him come to the therapist with me, and I confronted him. I felt a release of my anger for a while, but it eventually came back. He never seemed to change. I finally just gave up.

When I was thirty-two years old, I first learned of the three principles I have been talking about in this book. My whole life began a transformation—my work was rejuvenated, my stress level dropped dramatically, I found my true love (and married her), and my friendships changed and grew. The last area of my life to change was with my dad. I kept wondering why, if everything else could change, was my relationship with my dad so persistently difficult?

Then one day, I was driving up the driveway to my parents' house (my parents were now in their seventies). My stomach began to knot up and my thoughts began to swarm. "Here we go again," I thought. "Another disappointing visit with my dad. I'll say this, he'll say that, and we'll end up in an argument, me hurt and he rejecting." I was filled with thoughts of dread. Then, like a lightbulb going off in my head, I realized that it was all happening in my thoughts. I started to laugh uncontrollably. My wife looked at me and said, "What's going on with you?"

I regained my composure for a moment and responded, "I can't believe it's all happening in my thinking. He's not even here and I've already had a terribly disappointing visit with my dad and it all happened in my thoughts." I couldn't believe the power of my own thinking to create my experience. "Could it be that the entire thing with my dad was all in my head?" I sheepishly pondered. After all that therapy and years of torment, could it be that simple?

I wondered what would happen when I went into the house. Would my new understanding hold? I walked in and he was on the phone. I noticed my habitual thoughts taking that personally: "He's ignoring me again." But then I found it amusing that I would take that personally.

When he got off the phone, he threw out a big hunk of bait for me to bite on. "So," he said, "what did you think of what the peanut farmer did this week?" (He was referring to then-president Jimmy Carter.) Usually, he would goad me into political arguments and I would react—that was our game. But this time I just let it go by.

He then lobbed an even larger piece of bait right in front of my nose. "Those Democrats have no clue how to run a country." Again, I could see my old habit of reacting, but I almost felt as though I were hovering above myself observing myself reacting, but having a choice. It was all quite amusing to me, and I quietly giggled inside. After several rounds of this, he could see he wasn't going to get my normal reaction. Then he really shocked me.

"Do you want to play a game of gin?" he asked.

Shocked because he never asked me to play cards with him, I replied, "Sure." We played for two hours and had a great time. From that moment on, I saw my dad in a whole new light. I realized he was a very shy person who didn't know how to have a relationship with his sons that wasn't full of sarcasm, jabs, and left-handed humor. He was trying to love us; he just didn't know how. Years of my taking his actions personally had made it even worse, because he became uncomfortable around me and my constant challenging of his beliefs. For the first time, I saw his innocence.

From that day on, my relationship with him did a 180. We began to have a very enjoyable and close relationship and continued to do so until the time of his death thirteen years later. Essentially, what happened was that I forgave him. In realizing that my reactions to him came from my thinking, I saw his innocence and had a change of heart. All the anger and disappointment disappeared in an instant and never returned. He didn't completely stop being shy and awkward with me; I just saw it differently and didn't react. The past didn't change, but my understanding of it did. I understood not only his innocence, but the innocence of all of us.

Forgiveness is understanding the past from the viewpoint of separate, thought-created realities. Instead of taking everyone very personally, we see that we all get caught up in our ego-self thought system and act on those misconceptions of life.

# Why Forgive?

Why should we forgive? Most people think the reason we forgive others is because it is our religious or moral obligation or to let the other person off the hook and improve our relationship.

We don't really see what's in it for *us* to forgive.

Forgiveness is a good idea for several reasons.

1. It gives us the experience of the natural Self—timeless love.
2. It releases us from emotional pain, anger, resentment, and guilt.

3. It improves our physical health.
4. It allows us to love more fully and enjoy life.
5. It heals relationships and allows us to see others in a new light. We see our connection and unity with them.
6. It allows us to live in the present moment.

The one who forgives is the one who receives the greatest benefit from forgiveness. When we forgive, we let *ourselves* off the hook. We no longer have to live with the constant nagging thoughts of resentment. It doesn't feel good to carry resentment or guilt; it's not supposed to! This is our emotional guidance system at work. These sensations are there, just like physical pain, to warn us that something is out of balance—something needs to change.

Holding on to anger, resentment, or guilt is more than emotionally uncomfortable: it eats away at our insides. Numerous medical studies show the relationship of many diseases to unresolved emotions and thoughts of anger and resentment. High blood pressure, heart disease, certain types of cancer, intestinal disorders, and many other illnesses are listed as being highly related to negative emotional states. When we forgive, our body is in a better state of balance. We have more energy, our immune system is stronger, and we heal more quickly.

You can see unforgivingness in people's faces and bodies. They look lifeless and pained. But when people forgive, they appear to drop years from their faces. Unforgivingness makes us old more quickly. We feel the weight of the world on our shoulders when we don't forgive.

It is also good to forgive because it opens up our hearts to love fully. When we carry hurt, anger, resentment or guilt, we block that channel where love can flow freely. I once heard a Hawaiian story about this. The ancient legend is that each of us comes into the world with a bowl of light. This light is our joy, wisdom, and happiness. Each time

### ○ UNFORGIVENESS BLOCKS THE FLOW OF TIMELESS LOVE

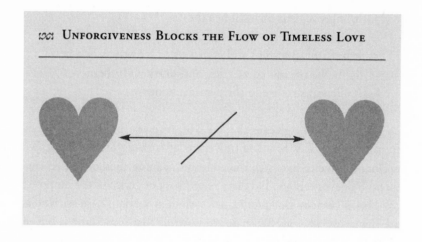

we carry a negative thought of the past in our mind, we place a stone in the bowl. With each stone, the light becomes dimmer and dimmer. Eventually, the light can go out and we lose touch with the wisdom, joy, and love that is the light in the bowl. Forgiveness is turning the bowl over and dumping out the stones. This applies to forgiving ourselves as well as others.

It is common to experience hurt, anger, jealousy, and all the emotions. Forgiveness is the gift to release these emotions. It unburdens us, it heals a broken heart, it restores love between people, it lets us love again.

### Lack of Forgiveness Blocks Love

○

I once met a man who was severely abused by his mother as a child, and he hated her all of his life. The more he hated her, the more he drank, as a way to medicate and anesthetize his emotional state. He eventually became an alcoholic, and though he went through treatment fifteen times and had short periods of sobriety, he would always relapse. His relapses always occurred when he would begin thinking again about his mom and the abuse. Something would always come along that would trigger those memories, and he just couldn't stand the pain of the anger. So he would drink, even though he knew clearly that it was killing him.

Then he went to treatment for the sixteenth time, this time in a center based on Health Realization, and he learned about the power of Thought to create his reality, his past, and his emotions. When he saw the relationship of his thinking to his behavior, he forgave himself. Then he saw his mother's own innocence, how she was abused by her parents and had never resolved her emotions about it. He saw that she was just like him. At that point, he forgave her, and with his act of forgiveness his thirst for alcohol went away. By forgiving her, he could maintain his sobriety, and he could love for the first time. He became a very selfless, giving person, helping other alcoholics and young people.

Another reason to forgive is that it heals our relationships. Our relationships with others exist in our minds—and are made up of all the thoughts we have about them. When we have a change of heart and see other people differently, we have different thoughts about them. When I saw my dad differently, our relationship did a 180-degree turn. He didn't need to change. I didn't even tell him that I forgave him. My thoughts just changed about him, and I realized that there was nothing to forgive. As a result, my perception of him and how I behaved with him changed. Understandably, he began to change too and was more relaxed around me. Our relationship healed and became very enjoyable.

When we forgive others, we open our hearts to them again. We see their humanness, their innocence, and their innate health. That doesn't mean we necessarily interact with them, however. Some people continue to be abusive, physically or psychologically, and the wise thing to do is to move on. But to really move on, we need to forgive. Otherwise, we carry the emotional baggage of that relationship with us.

In a relationship based on timeless love, forgiveness is a daily occurrence. We must keep dumping out the emotional stones so that the light can shine. When we forgive, we open the channel to love.

I still get angry with my wife from time to time, and she gets angry with me. But we could no more hang on to the anger than we could hang on to a burning coal. We can't because we know where the pain is coming from—not the other person, but our hanging on to the hot coal. Dropping it is the only choice.

Lastly, forgiveness allows us to live in the present moment. By not forgiving, we are constantly reminded of the past, and our thoughts dwell on memories of hurt. Forgiveness releases us from the bondage of the past and allows us to see life fresh in this moment. It lets us see the people we resented as they truly are in spirit rather than how they acted or how they were in our minds.

# Forgiveness: A New Way of Seeing

If timeless love is a river constantly flowing with feelings of gratitude, kindness, compassion, and joy, then resentment and unforgivingness is the dam that blocks that flow. When the water is dammed, it becomes polluted and contaminated. Forgiveness opens the floodgates and allows the water to flow again effortlessly. In flowing freely, the water is decontaminated, cleansing itself of the debris of the past. This clear water allows us to see the past with awareness. In my story of my relationship with my dad, once I saw his innocence, I saw the past in an entirely different way.

Another analogy for forgiveness is the wiper and washer for the windshield in your car. When we forgive we have a change of heart.

A change of heart is nothing more than looking at the same situation with a clean windshield. The negative view of life was not an absolute reality, just our dirty windshield. When we see clearly, we feel timeless love. When we see others as they are, with all their shortcomings and habits, we see beyond appearances to the innocence below the surface. We are all innocent, because we are all acting in every moment with the best thinking we are capable of in that moment. Certainly, we are all capable of better thinking and behavior than we sometimes exhibit, but nonetheless, it is the best we know to do in that instance.

## We Are All Innocent—An Extreme Case

We have a friend named Alec who is in prison for murder. My wife used to have an art studio across the hall from Alec's studio. They were friendly, but not close at the time. I had met him on a few occasions at art showings. One day after returning from a month-long trip out of the country, Michael had a message from his wife. She said she was moving things out of Alec's studio and wondered if Michael would be interested in some of his art supplies. It was then we found out that while we were out of town, his picture had been on the front page of the paper as a suspect in a brutal robbery and murder. Alec was such a friendly and kind person that we were sure there was some mistake.

We arranged for a Health Realization counselor to work with Alec in jail, and we developed a close relationship with Alec. After speaking with him while he was in jail awaiting trial, we came to understand that he had been depressed for months before the crime. However, we weren't free to speak to him about the crime. We knew he was part of the robbery but nothing more. Fortunately for us and his counselor, it wasn't necessary for us to know such details to share the principles of Health Realization.

Being in this horribly desperate situation, Alec listened as deeply as he could. At one point the therapist realized that he was guilty, and she helped him listen deeply to his heart. Midway through jury selection, Alec confessed to the crime. "Once he listened to his heart," his therapist said, "he didn't have a choice. It was the only thing he could do."

I can't condone what he did, and I do think he should pay in some way for the great hurt he caused. However, understanding the desperation of his thinking at the moment he committed the murder helped Michael and me understand how he could have done it. We could see his innocence as someone hopelessly embroiled in a misguided thought system, but nonetheless guilty of the crime.

As Alec gained an understanding of himself and the principles of Health Realization, he felt tremendous remorse for his act and wrote an extraordinary letter to the family of the victim and to his own family.

He read the letter in the courtroom, at the sentencing, and it touched everyone in the room, including the hardened bailiff. Alec was sincere because he also saw his own innocence and yet he was accountable for his actions. The district attorney commented that the reason he moved to a state that didn't have the death penalty was because of people like Alec.

Now Alec is in prison for many years, yet he is a free man, because he has found the source of his experience and his happiness. Through his past work as the editor of the prison newspaper, Alec printed material on Health Realization for fellow prisoners. He was a great teacher to both Michael and me in seeing innocence in someone who has committed the ultimate act of insecurity.

# The Process of Forgiveness

The following will serve as a guide to prepare you for forgiveness as well as a breakdown of the process of forgiveness. You may be convinced of the power and value of forgiveness, yet still seem unable to forgive. The following guidelines will help prepare you for forgiveness and see you through the process.

- See the value of forgiveness for yourself and others.
- Be willing to forgive.
- Recognize your unforgiving thinking and let it go.
- See the innocence in others.
- Accept the humanness of your unforgiving thoughts.

### See the Value of Forgiveness for Yourself and Others

Understanding that forgiveness is good for your health, your emotional well-being, and your wholeness paves the way for opening yourself to forgiving. Knowing that the source of your experience is your power to think, and that the power of Consciousness makes those thoughts real, breaks the spell of blaming others for your present emotions. You can't make yourself forgive; it is an expression of the spiritual Self. But you can be open to it. Don't judge how fast or slow your process is; just accept where you are at the time.

### Be Willing to Forgive

Just being willing to forgive opens you up to the possibility of a change of heart. Not too long ago, I experienced a very painful disappointment in someone close to me. I felt angrier than I had in many years. It felt awful. I couldn't sleep well for many days. I knew where my anger was coming from—my thinking—but I just couldn't seem to get over it as quickly as I usually do. I was willing to have a change of heart. I knew it would come, I just didn't know when.

On the fourth night of this crisis, I woke up at 2:30 in the morning. I felt a surge of compassion for the person I was angry at. I saw him as a young child, even though he is now quite old. I could see his fear and his motivation for his unsavory behavior. A great feeling of peace and compassion came over me. I felt so grateful for my change of heart. It didn't make me weak or foolish; I still knew how to protect myself from him. But I no longer had the anger.

### Recognize Your Unforgiving Thinking and Let It Go

While you are waiting for the insight that will allow you to forgive another, you will still have unforgiving thoughts. Something that person does or something someone else does will remind you of what you are resentful about.

When these thoughts come to mind, don't fight them or repress them. Just see them as thoughts, and accept your humanness for having them. Also notice the emotions you are having. If you get angry or sad or any emotion, just acknowledge it, which will create the space for you to let it go. Remember that the past does not exist now; only the memory of it exists in your thoughts as a virtual reality. See these thoughts of the past as debris floating down the river. Don't pull them out to inspect them or analyze them, just acknowledge these thoughts and let them pass by.

When I was still angry with the person I mentioned in the previous section, I was bombarded with thoughts of this individual from time to time. Sometimes I got caught up in the thoughts and would forget that I was doing the thinking, but eventually I would wake up to my thinking and it would pass. I accepted this as part of the forgiving process.

### See the Innocence in Others

Seeing innocence is remembering that people are doing what makes sense to them at the time through the filter of their own thinking. Their actions may be based on fear, insecurity, and their own unresolved issues. Whatever the reason, it makes sense in their personal reality. All of us get caught up in our thinking, no matter how stupid, unwise, destructive, or crazy it may be. Remembering that, and giving people the benefit of the doubt, will help you to see their innocence. Giving them the benefit of the doubt, however, does not mean that you assume they did nothing. It means that given their level of understanding at the time, with all of its misconceptions and beliefs, they were doing the best they could. It means that their belief system only allowed certain options.

Even if people are intentionally and consciously hurting you, it is still because they are lost in their thinking. They have lost awareness of their connection with Universal Love (Mind). When I just observe these people without judging and realize that I may not understand their logic or their intentions, that thought keeps me from ascribing intentions and motives to their behavior. How often have I interpreted something someone has done as something that person has done "to me," only later to find out it had nothing to do with me at all.

A good friend once told me of being very angry with a driver on the freeway who cut him off to save some precious moments. Later, my friend, who was taking his daughter to the doctor, saw this same man getting out of his car, and my friend's anger resurged. He walked up to the man and accusingly said, "Don't you realize that by cutting people off, you risk their lives and yours?"

The man apologized profusely and said, "I was just called by my doctor and told to get right into the hospital, that the results of my cancer tests had just come in and he needed to talk to me right away. I was frightened of the possibility, and in my fear I was careless in my driving. I am very sorry."

My friend learned a very important lesson that day. He said, "I never really know what motivates another person's behavior, no matter how rude it may appear. I will give others the benefit of the doubt more readily in the future."

Seeing innocence doesn't mean that you don't listen to your common sense if you need to protect yourself from danger or hold someone accountable for his or her behavior. But observing without judgment helps you to discern if there is real danger or if you are ascribing intentions and motives to the other person.

## Accept the Humanness of Your Unforgiving Thoughts

Too often we get down on ourselves for not forgiving. We may think, "I should be able to move beyond this. Why am I letting that person ruin my life? I feel guilty for staying angry when I should be forgiving." Getting down on yourself for thinking anything will just make it stick around longer. It's like trying to not think of having a cigarette when you are quitting smoking. The more you try not to think about it, the more you do think about it. Accepting your thinking and your emotions and then letting them pass allows you to heal from a past hurt more quickly.

This last story will illustrate the process of forgiveness. In the previous chapter, Lydia and Dan began their healing process with a heart-to-heart talk. For most couples with more serious issues like infidelity, forgiveness is not completed in one heart-to-heart, but occurs over time in gradual layers of forgiveness. The following story took place in another therapy session, a year and a half after their first talk about the affair. Lydia and Dan's story will illustrate how one couple moved into a change of heart that led to forgiveness.

### The Wounded Heart Heals

ʂʘʂ

Lydia spoke to Dan from her heart. "The real moment when I realized that forgiveness was happening was when we were lying in bed and you were telling me that you were still in pain about having the one-night stand. I could feel, at a very deep level, how intense your pain was about this. It was not a good thing for you to feel. I felt such compassion for you. At that moment I knew it was over for me to feel any more resentment. I literally felt my heart shift. For me it was gone. Now I can think about the infidelity and it is just a memory—it is no longer an emotional experience. It is like someone else's story."

Lydia continued, now turning to me, "Before forgiveness occurred, it was all about me—my hurt, my pain, his betrayal of my trust. I felt like I deserved to be angry, to feel sorry for myself, that I had the 'right' to be indignant and self-righteous. Now I know that it is forgiven and that term is appropriate—for-give, given away. I'm no longer interested in hanging on to the resentment and self-pity. I want to give it away. When I get mad at him for something else, the memory of the infidelity may still come up in my mind, but it has no emotional charge, it is no longer a weapon to hit him with."

"What led up to the moment when your heart shifted?" I asked Lydia.

"I can't explain it except to say, I didn't like the way I felt all the time." She reflected, "I didn't like walking around in that state of aggression, this constant 'pus wound' that was always being set off. I saw that I didn't like it. That was the first step—to get sick of feeling the unforgivingness. Then I became resolved that I was going to let it go. It didn't let go immediately, but it did set the stage for forgiveness to occur. There was a real desire to move beyond this, whether Dan and I stay together or not, I needed to move past being unforgiving. It would continue to wound me in my relationship with Dan or any future relationship if we ended ours. I need to be able to trust again."

"That's another thing," Lydia recalled. "I had always lived with the belief that infidelity was out of the question for me, and therefore I believed it was out of the question for Dan, as well. He couldn't possibly be unfaithful to me if he loved me! But he did and I was devastated. I felt so betrayed. I loved living in an innocent state of trusting and I hated living in a state of mistrust. I knew I wanted to live my life in a state of trust again, because I truly like that. That set the stage for forgiveness to occur.

"I realized that whether I live my life in a state of mistrust or in a state of trust, I can be betrayed. Either way people can lie to you or betray you, but that doesn't dictate whether or not I live my life in a state of trust or mistrust. I choose to live in a state of trust for my own sake, regardless of what Dan or anyone does. It's for me, for my own sanity. I realized that I had to do it for me, not him. I hope it helps him, but I didn't do it for that."

Lydia's realization that peace could only come from within herself resulted in unconditional forgiveness. She proceeded, "The other thing was that once forgiveness flooded my heart, I had room for him again in my life. Prior to that I had shut him out emotionally for two years. We were living parallel lives, but there was no feeling of intimacy. From the moment that I forgave him, there was room again for him in my life. Before that it was all me, me, me. There was more space in my heart for him. I felt compassion for him because he still hasn't forgiven himself."

Lydia now understood in her heart what, a year before, had been an ideal concept. "Forgiveness really isn't about forgiving a specific transgression or event, it is moving into a space of forgiveness. It's not about the specifics, it's about a feeling that sets you free from the details. And that's the moving beyond part. I truly moved beyond the anger and resentment, into a *feeling* of forgiveness."

"When Lydia's heart shifted, I felt free to express my pain about the infidelity," Dan responded. "Before that, there was no room for me to share my feelings; Lydia couldn't have heard me. After her heart shifted, I knew she completely understood where I was coming from. I felt her compassion. There was no judgment from her and I felt free to speak from my heart."

"I know you really heard me and were compassionate to me," Dan told Lydia. "When you were in that state of forgiveness, I felt your total acceptance and we finally reconnected. The details no longer mattered; they washed away."

Dan looked at both of us and said, "It was a relief to share my feelings with her and that helped me begin to forgive myself, though that process is not yet complete for me. Right now I am still back and forth about forgiving myself, it depends on my mood. I am where Lydia was earlier in her process. I haven't yet fully had a change of heart about myself, but I want it and am open to change. It just hasn't happened yet. It comes in waves. Sometimes I seem to have let it go and then there is another wave that comes like a cesspool of guilt and shame. I am sick of it. I get angry with myself for not letting it go because it is robbing me and us of a life together. But, I know that I will and I have hope. That makes it better."

This is not the end of their story. Like all relationships, Dan and Lydia are in a process of becoming love. They are discovering how to be present and live from their natural Selves—the true remedy to relationship problems. The infidelity wasn't the problem; it was just the symptom.

Dan still needs to accept himself and all of his feelings and emotions. He is impatient with the healing/forgiveness process. It is only when we accept ourselves, where we are, that the paradox of transformation occurs. When we accept and embrace our pain, it goes away. When we fight it and try to make it go away, it stays. In Chapter 10, we will talk about the process of becoming love and the need for wholehearted acceptance to move beyond where we are in any moment or phase of our relationship or our lives.

I hope this chapter has helped you to understand the need for forgiveness and how you can move into its state. The more you forgive, the more you will see how light it makes you feel. The less stubborn you are about forgiving, the more strength you will find. Forgiving is not a sign of weakness but of true strength. When you see forgiveness as a way of life, you will live in the moment more in your relationships, and you will see them transform and evolve. You will also be able to love fully and wholeheartedly, and you will experience timeless love.

# 9

# TRANSFORMING CONFLICT INTO WHOLEHEARTED RESOLUTION

❖——❖

*Mankind cannot solve its problems at the level of thinking that created those problems.*

—ALBERT EINSTEIN

ONE OF THE by-products of our fast-paced modern society is an increased level of irritation, anger, violence, and conflict. We see this lack of awareness of the natural Self on a global level in ever-increasing wars, ethnic and religious tensions, school violence like Columbine, terrorist attacks, drive-by shootings, gang-related violence, workplace homicides, child abuse, and family violence. Even in nonviolent acts, such as waiting in line at airports, in stores, and on the highway, we witness daily evidence of impatience; a lack of courtesy; and a self-centered, self-righteous sense of inhumanity.

We seem to be in a collective low mood. When observed in the light of what we have spoken of in this book, this lowering of collective consciousness makes total sense. What other kind of mood could we possibly experience when we ignore our true feelings and live our lives in a state of perpetual imbalance and fear? We are so speeded up that we neither see nor heed the warnings of the instrument panel of our feelings and emotions, which could otherwise guide us back to the sanity of the speed of love. We live more enmeshed in the world of the ego-self and more removed from the world of the natural Self.

Our intimate relationships are no exception to this trend. As a matter of fact, they are usually the first area to feel the impact of a speeded-up life that is out of balance. When we are out of balance, we are more easily bothered by our partner's habits and idiosyncrasies. We take everything our mate does more personally, which leads to thoughts and the experience of hurt and anger and potential conflict.

The purpose of this chapter is to help you find a way to deal with conflict in your significant relationships. We will explore the causes of conflict; our moods; traditional ways of resolving conflict that haven't been successful; and a method of conflict resolution that is natural, loving, and leads to a win-win solution for all parties. The approach I offer will not only reduce the level of conflict, but will also transform conflict into an opportunity for wholehearted resolution and an ever-deepening experience of timeless love. This wholehearted resolution model will combine everything you have learned in this book thus far: the natural Self versus the ego-self, the three principles of human experience, separate realities, our inner guidance system, deep listening, presence, heart-to-heart communication, and forgiveness. In a sense, this chapter will put it all together in a practical way that will be applicable to your life and your relationships.

# Causes of Conflict

As I said earlier, many of us do not live in a world that moves at the timeless speed of love. Instead, we live in a time-bound world—where we are in a hurry, stressed out, impatient, irritable, and out of balance. In short, we do not live from the awareness of the natural Self. This imbalance puts us in a state of mind that is like a fight waiting to happen. Have you ever been in that mood where you are just waiting for your mate or someone else to say something that will trigger your wrath? As Clint Eastwood said in the movie *Sudden Impact*, "Go ahead, make my day!" Or, if you are less prone to anger, have you ever found yourself just waiting for something awful to happen to you?

## *Unrecognized Low Moods*

One of the major causes of conflict in relationships is an unrecognized low mood. A low mood is not a mysterious fog that comes over you indiscriminately or something you catch like a cold. It is a label that has been commonly used to explain a level of behavior. A low mood, in truth, is a low level of awareness. At that low level of consciousness, you are unaware of your true nature and your connection to timeless love. It is important to bring up this point early in our discussion of moods to demystify them. To transform your low mood, you must take responsibility, and accept and embrace the low mood in timeless love. When you wait until your mind is quiet and you have regained the balance of timeless love before acting on your thinking, you will save yourself and your partner the stress and anxiety that come from a low-mood interaction. It is then that you will see what adjustments, if any, you need to make to accommodate your present situation.

Here is how a low mood exerts its influence. When we are in a low mood, we see life through our painful past memories and habits—the ego-self belief system. In the Dr. Jekyll and Mr. Hyde story, a low mood would be our Mr. Hyde—the dark side. If we don't know we are in a low mood, we will trust our distorted perceptions and act on them, bringing pain and conflict to our relationships.

We will explore the concept of moods more fully a little later in this chapter. In the meantime, let's explore the other causes of conflict in relationships.

## Conflicting Needs, Wants, and Desires

A second cause of conflict in relationships is conflicting needs, wants, and desires. From the separated self of the ego, we falsely believe that life is a win-lose proposition, and that there is no such thing as a win-win solution. We must get our way; otherwise, we will not get our needs met. We see the fulfillment of our needs as dependent on the one special person in our lives. The fear that this person will not meet our needs leads to conflict and a feeling of dependency.

As we learned in the first chapter on the nature of timeless love, we are the love we seek, and we live in an abundant world that is just not yet visible at our present level of consciousness. When we are living from a place of timeless love, as the natural Self, we see that there is no winning or losing, only gain. But as the ego-self, we see ourselves as separate from our mate, rather than in unity or oneness with that person.

When we look outside for love instead of recognizing that we are love, we create a feeling of neediness. Kris and Mike, the couple I spoke about in Chapter 2, looked to each other to fill up the emptiness that they felt. They were so happy being in love; that is, until they failed to live up to each other's expectations. That's when their love turned to hatred, disappointment, and fear. But when they rediscovered the true source of love—from within—they recaptured the essence of timeless love.

## *Conflicting Values and Beliefs*

A third cause of conflict in relationships is conflicting values and beliefs. These could be our beliefs about being on time, our financial values, religious and political beliefs, work ethics, parenting styles, family traditions, and an infinite number of other differences. As you learned in Chapter 5, we all live in a thought-created separate reality. When we are unaware of this fact of human nature, our differences become a source of conflict, disappointment, and hurt. Of course, when we understand and are aware of the principle of separate realities in the moment, our differences enrich us and do not cause irresolvable conflict. We can talk out these differences in a heart-to-heart manner, which can lead each person to insights and an expanded view of life. Unfortunately, most people are not aware of separate realities. If they were, we wouldn't have the enormous conflict that we presently have in the world.

## *Need for Power and Control*

A fourth cause of conflict is the need for power and control. When we think fearful thoughts, we seek power and control. Fear is born of the separated self. It stems from the illusion that we are separate and does not recognize that we are united in spirit and one with Universal Mind. If we need to think we are right, smarter than, stronger than, or morally superior to someone else, we are really expressing our level of fear and insecurity. The more fearful a person is, the more important power and control is to that person.

When we don't have a sense of safety, we seek power and control. However, the only true condition of safety comes from being at one with our spiritual Self and not from any external factors (such as guns, physical strength, or political or economic control). Many couples live with the tyranny of control—they are in a constant tug-of-war over who is in control. When we realize that nothing of any true value can ever be taken from us, there is no need to control. When we let go of fear and accept the ultimate power of love in our lives, we are free from control. Many prisoners have discovered true freedom from behind bars, which are the ultimate form of external control, when they discovered the source of their experience.

As you can already surmise, all of these causes of conflict are really just different forms of one and the same cause—the illusion of operating from our unrecognized ego-self. Another result of operating from the insecurity of our ego's belief system is low moods. We will now address how to deal effectively with low moods.

## Moods

Moods are one of the most common causes of conflict in our relationships. Understanding moods is as necessary to relationships as is checking the weather before we dress for the day. What we wear doesn't change the weather; it just makes it easier to be comfortable in it. The same is true for understanding moods. While interviewing couples for this book, they all stated that understanding moods helped solve the majority of their conflicts.

Moods are the ups and downs of our daily existence. In actuality, moods are the experience of moving in and out of our natural Self and ego-self—they are the fluctuations in the quality of our thinking. When our mood changes, we move on a continuum between balance in a high mood and imbalance in a low mood. Our high moods are characterized by true feelings of joy, lightheartedness, compassion for others, energy, hope, gratitude, and happiness. Our low moods are characterized by thoughts and emotions of pessimism, depression, self-pity, self-doubt, fear, worry, resentment, anger, obsessive thinking coupled with anxiety, and a variety of other uncomfortable emotions.

Our perception of daily life changes, often dramatically, when we are in different moods. For example, when I am in a high mood I am filled with a sense of ease in my relationship—love, gratitude for my mate, humor, and appreciation of our differences. However, these same differences that I loved in a high mood are what I judge, resent, or am bothered by in a low mood. For instance, when I am in a low mood, Michael's method of describing a concept or issue seems too detailed and I become impatient. My impatience is a sign to me to listen more deeply. In a high mood I find her very creative and deep. I know now (at least I usually do) not to take these perceptions to heart when I am in a low mood. Instead, I just wait for the storm to pass.

The following diagram illustrates high and low moods and how they affect our emotional state, our perceptions, and our attitude.

When we recognize our moods and those of others, it is common sense to reevaluate how serious we are taking our thinking. When Mark

## ∞ QUALITY OF THINKING

*High Mood (Natural Self)*

EXPRESSION OF TRUE FEELINGS

*Ease • Joy • Loving • Happy • Creative • Hopeful • Caring • Compassionate • Rolling with the Punches*

*Low Mood (Ego-Self)*

EXPRESSION OF FEARFUL THOUGHTS
AND EMOTIONS

*Pessimistic • Taking Things Personally • Angry • Resentful • Self-Doubt • Self-Pity • Depressed • Stressed • Fearful*

gets irritated with Karla's side of the closet, as we discussed in Chapter 5, he knows that the irritation is his signal that his mood is off at that moment. He now has an awareness that he is in a low mood, and he knows not to take his thinking seriously.

How do we recognize a low mood? If we notice that we are caught up in a flurry of negative emotions, it may mean that our mood is off. If we are wise, we will step back and listen deeply. This pause to reflect allows us to take our mood pulse and know if we should reconsider our thinking. When our mind is clear we will discern what is an appropriate response. For example, yesterday I had a beautiful day at my cabin. I wrote in the morning, did some chores, and then went cross-country skiing. It was a spectacularly sunny day, and I saw some wolf tracks and a moose on the shore as I passed. My mood (my level of consciousness) was very high, and I was filled with feelings of awe, gratitude, and joy. After lunch I did some carpentry work inside the cabin. Later in the afternoon, I noticed that nothing was going right. I was making lots of mistakes in my measurements and was feeling impatient, irritable, and tired. I reflected for a moment and realized I was tired and decided to quit working for the day. I could have pushed on to finish the project, but instead I listened to myself. This minor fluctuation in my mood was nothing more than being tired and ignoring the wisdom of that sensation for a while. Once I heard it, I changed what I was doing, and my high mood returned.

Mood management is a matter of moving from awareness to acceptance to reevaluation to adjustment. We become aware that we are in a low mood and have lost our awareness of timeless love. We refrain from judgment and accept ourself and what we are experiencing and reevaluate our low mood thinking. Our common sense will return and we will know what appropriate action to take, if any. Listening within to our needs and respecting them leads to less time spent in low moods. Many low moods are caused in part by physical imbalance—hunger, a need for rest, pacing, illness, nutritional imbalance, and exercise.

Of course, at times our true feelings and emotions will let us know that something is off in our relationship or our circumstances, something that is not mood-related. We will discuss how to deal with those relationship issues in the section on wholehearted resolution. For now, let us return to the topic of moods and how to deal with other people's low moods.

Sometimes your mood seems to be just fine, but your partner is in a low mood. How do you immunize yourself from "catching" your partner's low mood, and how do you keep your bearings with someone who is in a low mood? The answer is quite simple: don't take it personally; it's not about you. Some people take the weather personally, but weather is just weather; it doesn't care how you react. The same is true for moods. Having high and low moods is part of life. Taking your low moods personally or other people's low moods personally is optional. When we do take moods personally, we feel guilty, hurt, angry, disappointed, controlling, impatient, and a host of other negative emotions. If I am crabby and tired, I may take it out on Michael by being oppositional. She, in turn, can react with anger, or, simply see it as a low mood. All of these emotional reactions are indications of a low mood and a state of imbalance. You may choose to blame the other person for your low mood, but as we discussed in Chapter 5, the truth is that you create your own experience through the principle of Thought.

When you recognize someone else's low mood and are able to keep your bearings (stay in your natural Self), you will automatically feel a sense of compassion and understanding. After all, who hasn't been in a low mood? Sometimes it is difficult to be with someone in this state for a long time, but that depends on whether or not you keep your bearings, don't take it personally, and feel compassion. Compassion is like an antibiotic for the low-mood virus.

When Michael is in a low mood and I am in my natural Self, I feel so much compassion for her. I naturally want to comfort her if I can and if she is willing to receive the comfort. Sometimes I need to just leave her alone and accept her low mood. Other times it seems really funny to me—it's as though she is temporarily playing a villain in a play. On occasion sharing that point of view with her helps her see the humor of it too, but at other times, I am wise to keep my humor to myself. The bottom line is that I can only catch her low mood if I forget that the source of my experience is my thinking.

Often, it may appear as if you are catching your partner's low mood because you are in a kind of gray zone. In that state, your mood is not very high, but you're not in a low mood either; at least that's your perception of the situation. This zone, being neither black nor white, can be confusing. You have a low tolerance but you don't know it. You thought you were in a good mood but are starting to get clues to the contrary, like becoming easily bothered or judgmental. If your partner is in a low mood and you are having difficulty putting it in perspective and not taking it personally, you may be in the gray zone. Don't judge yourself; just accept that you are not in as good a place as you thought. Your mind will quiet, and you will see what to do.

Here is a story (in their own words) of two people who were both in a low mood at the same time. For most couples, this is a combination that often ends in an argument, but for Rick and Pamela, it ended in a good laugh.

### The Household Chore Blues

ᛞᛞᛞ

It was one of those weekend days where we had a million chores to do around the house. I was busy hanging curtain rods and Rick was trying to connect all the stereo components in our new surround sound system. Curtains, curtain rods, tools, wires, and boxes were all over the living room. After the fourth time of drilling the hole in the wrong place for the curtain rod holder, I lost it. I was sure Rick would be upset with me, because the wall was looking like someone had taken a machine gun to it. I knew we were in trouble when I started hearing a series of four-letter words in surround sound, except they weren't coming from the speakers.

"This damn wire won't go where it's supposed to. Why do they make these [blankety-blank] instructions so difficult?" Rick seethed under his breath.

I knew we were about to have a fight. I could feel it brewing. Then, he commented on my feeble attempts to find the stud in the wall.

"Can't you hang curtain rods without destroying our house!" Rick shouted. He was now visibly losing it.

For a moment I felt like reacting. The words of rebuttal ran through my mind, but luckily I realized that both our moods were approaching meltdown status. Instead, I said, "I think we need a break. Let's not let this ruin our day. How about it, Mr. Wizard?"

Rick laughed and saw the absurdity of our situation. His mood shifted enough to see the futility of continuing. Instead he said, "Yes, let's just blow it off and come back to it tomorrow, when we're both in a better frame of mind." We dropped what we were doing and took our two children out to build a snowman and had a great time. The next day we did go back to our projects, and it was smooth sailing all the way. What could have ended in an argument and a ruined day turned into a family day with the kids. The jobs still got done, but we didn't let them ruin our weekend together.

When we understand moods, we remove most of the conflict in our relationships. How do we deal with our differences in a way that leads to unity and intimacy, rather than separation and distance? We will now explore two of the common models human beings have used to deal with conflict and a new model of wholehearted resolution, which will be rooted in the natural Self.

# The Power-Control Mode of Conflict Resolution

One common solution to dealing with our differences is to try to get our way. This model assumes that one of us will get his or her way, so it might as well be me.

Within the power-control model of conflict resolution many levels of consciousness exist. At the lowest level, awareness is relatively nonexistent; power and control are accomplished through threats and physical force. Overpowering someone with physical strength is used in parent/child, male/female, and many other relationships. Physical force is never acceptable in any circumstances. The more common forms of power-control are emotional/intellectual manipulation in the form of persuasion, guilt, debate, logical reasoning, and group pressure. These nonphysical approaches are the current, socially acceptable forms that range from obvious attempts at control to more covert methods.

We are often unaware of the potential subtleties of this model. For instance, we may not realize that we are trying to manipulate someone or that we are being manipulated. Awareness is the key.

We learn the habit of subtle manipulation early in our development. Like a fish in water, it is totally out of our awareness. People are engaged in the so-called art of manipulation more than they think; it is an integral part of daily life. Plenty of examples are all around us, although our minds may be too preoccupied or conditioned to notice. An obvious example is advertising and the media. These forms of manipulation represent the level of consciousness of our society; we've created them and in turn advertising and the media influence and teach us how to subtly manipulate each other and ourselves unconsciously.

For an illustration of hidden manipulation, you need go no further than yourself. You are constantly using your ego-belief system to try to talk yourself into and out of things. For example, you might say to yourself, "Yes, you should go to that party; you'll hurt his feelings if you don't. What will he think? He'll think you don't care." Or, "No, don't be honest, don't say what you feel. She might dump you."

It's interesting how we unknowingly manipulate ourselves. We constantly talk ourselves out of listening to our inner feelings and being our natural Selves.

Although Michael and I appreciate watching old movies from the 1940s and 1950s with my ninety-two-year-old mom, we often laugh and say, "No wonder everyone in our generation is so confused about relationships. Look what was handed down from the generations before." Movies copy life, and life copies movies. We are always amused by these lightweight love stories portraying the same theme, "the battle of the sexes," as it was once called. The male or female connives to win the attention of the opposite sex, to keep that person's attention, to get his or her way in the relationship, to get the mink coat, to go on the hunting trip. The heroes and heroines condone their behavior by saying, "All's fair in love and war." It is the ultimate excuse in the socially acceptable game of the egos.

The newer movies aren't any better as role models or as raisers of our awareness. They contain the same notions of control but played out with a great deal of sophisticated presentation. In the old movies, manipulation looks obvious to us, but in the present time we haven't really changed much. Some of us may be a little more honest in our relationships, but in reality we still play games of power and control. We are in a new century; we have honed our skills of guilt and manipulation to the slick sophistication of a New York ad agency. That makes the games no more obvious to us than they were to our parents or grandparents. Either way, if we play the game of life from the standpoint of the ego, there are no winners.

The forms of the power/control model of conflict resolution are endless, but all are based on these assumptions:

1. There is not enough _____ (power, money, affection, you fill in the blank) to go around.
2. I need to control others to get my way.
3. Some win, some lose.
4. I deserve this; I have a right to it.

This model has led to thousands of years of wars, conflicts, and human misery. As we have evolved as a society and culture, we still continue to use the power/control model, but we now have a more advanced, civil way—compromise.

# The Compromise Model of Conflict Resolution

The compromise model of conflict resolution is based on the assumption that we can avoid conflict if each of us gets part of his or her way. Compromise appears to lead to fewer arguments, is more civil, and at least you get some of what you want and need. Like the power-control model, this is also based on the assumption that there is not enough for everyone, but rather than fight for your needs, you learn to give and take. When people in a relationship come to an impasse, compromise has worked better than constant fighting, with only one winner and always one loser. After all, "half a loaf is better than no loaf."

There's one major problem with this model, however. The compromise model undermines the integrity of our natural Self. Think about it. Your true feelings are your guidance system. If you were taught that to have a happy marriage you must sometimes ignore your true feelings and compromise, you would be conflicted much of the time.

Another way in which the compromise model can undermine integrity is in its "you give me what I want and I will give you what you want" idea, which is akin to the "you scratch my back and I'll scratch yours" model of business and politics. History is proving that this process can undermine societal values and bring us down to the level of mediocrity and dishonesty without us even realizing it. The practice of compromise in the business and political arena puts undue pressure on individuals within that arena and brings their ego-belief systems into full play to rationalize their actions. They can't help but compromise the integrity of their true nature in the process. The same is true when we compromise our spirit in our personal relationships. Society and all the relationships that comprise it are directly affected by compromising our spiritual nature in any area of our life.

As clean as proponents of the compromise model try to present it, compromise often deteriorates into the methods of the power-control model. We use a lot of subtle manipulation, persuasion, guilt, debate, logical reasoning, and group pressure unknowingly to try to get our way.

In the following story, you'll see how the compromise model played out in the relationship of two of my friends, Piper and Victor.

### Compromise Versus Integrity

Victor had known, before he met Piper, that his purpose in life was to live in the awareness of his spiritual Self. His wish was to find someone who shared his spiritual dream, and he did—he met Piper. They had what seemed to be a great relationship, very loving, and based on the principles of Health Realization. But while they thought they had an understanding of how to have a heart-to-heart talk, many of their old issues were never resolved.

Victor's instincts and intuitions were very strong, but in his belief system was a live-and-let-live attitude that unknowingly interrupted the messages from his true feelings. He always wanted to respect Piper's wishes. As a result, if he was not completely sure about his true feeling, he would compromise. Piper, on the other hand, was more willing to argue for her belief system, thinking that her belief was as good as his was. But her attention span was short, and it was a little more difficult for her to listen deeply to Victor and her true feelings.

At this point in time, neither Piper nor Victor could read the subtle nuances of their feelings and emotions. Years passed, and although many areas of his life seemed fulfilled, Victor was experiencing the effects of compromising his spirit by not listening to his true feelings. Too many times he had let Piper's urgings take precedent over his intuition and sense of timing. He took on pressure from her expectations and fell out of touch with his spiritual nature. His life was speeded up, and he could feel the imbalance of too many activities and not enough time for reflection. He became more confused, and Piper became more moody. Then Victor temporarily moved out, but they chose to keep their relationship fully intact. In fact, they spent most of their time together. During this next year they saw a Health Realization counselor in hopes of understanding the principles of Mind, Thought, and Consciousness at a deeper level.

One day Victor was visiting with his mother-in-law, whom he deeply cared about. She rarely gave advice but wanted to offer him an insight into what she thought had been the cornerstone of her relationships. She said to Victor, with sweet concern, "Compromise is a good idea." That was all she said.

At that moment Victor could feel his true feelings surface. A voice inside him said, "Compromise has been the problem all along. I can't compromise my spirit any longer." Victor had seen in a flash how he had pushed his own true feelings aside and sacrificed his inner timing and balance again and again to keep peace. He saw his and Piper's innocence, how they both had let belief systems, which they had acquired early in life from well-intentioned people, influence how they saw reality and shut out their innate wisdom.

Victor and Piper passed that crossroad, and the lightness of their spirits resurfaced. They recommitted to a spiritual direction for their relationship. Their awareness of listening deeply to themselves and each other improved. In short, they experienced more timeless love. It was a win-win situation. Victor felt like he had rejoined his natural Self, and Piper now looks back on that time as a remarkable turning point for her. She is profoundly moved by her new awareness of listening deeply to herself and others. Now they are living a full and happy life together. They see that true resolution is not about resolving conflicts but about seeing that the truth that lies within each of us is the same.

Clearly, the compromise model has several downsides. Neither person gets exactly what he or she wants and needs; it is very tedious and time-consuming; it generally delays the conflict; both parties often feel resentment; and the conflict usually resurfaces again and again because of separate perceptions of what is "fair."

To truly resolve differences, we must look at the concept of conflict in a whole new way. We must give the creative nature of the spirit room to ingeniously turn differences into opportunities. As Albert Einstein so profoundly stated, "Mankind cannot solve its problems at the level of thinking that created those problems." If we truly understood what Einstein meant, we would seek to transcend the level at which the problem was created. We would see that power/control and compromise don't save time but take more time. We would not try so hard to preserve the status quo of the small details we often find so important, but instead would open ourselves to an as yet unknown bigger picture of life, one that unites our hearts and minds. In this bigger picture, the efficiency of a wholehearted approach would be apparent.

# The Wholehearted Model of Conflict Resolution

The third model is called the *wholehearted model of resolution* because it is based on the heart and mind being united. It is not a belief, a practice, or a technique, but a way of being that is natural.

When we are living as our natural Selves, we express love's boundless and harmonious qualities. We experience a clear mind and our thinking becomes more creative and filled with possibilities. Take for instance an artist, a songwriter, and a golfer; they all speak about how their creative moments come out of the blue, when they are "in the zone," or when they aren't caught up in their process thinking. Einstein attributed his ingenious discoveries to spirit. He was very clear that we have to rise above our belief system to create a new reality. Our possibilities are endless if we live from our true nature, rather than fear.

When we are fearful, we think that there is not enough to go around or we won't get our way. In timeless love we are abundant, creative, and prolific. We are able to let go of our rigid ways of doing things and we become more understanding of our partner's point of view. Instead of anger and blame, we experience true feelings of understanding and compassion. In this model, we see conflict as a temporary situation. It is a sign that we have momentarily slipped back into the reality of our ego-selves and that we can't see the obvious solution right under our noses.

There is no win-lose outcome in this model, only win-win. There is no need to compromise, because a solution neither party has yet considered transcends the limitations of our present thinking.

At times you will be surprised to find that the true solution to a problem may have nothing to do with the particulars of that problem. For instance, a friend of mine was astonished to discover what he thought was a slight struggle over a decision about whether or not he and his wife should drive to Chicago to visit friends, turned out to be an opportunity to transform the fabric of their relationship.

### The Silver Lining in a Relationship Cloud

*∞*

Connie was the instigator of the trip. She had talked to their friends and planned the details of what she thought would be a relaxing break in their hectic schedule. But Steve didn't know how much time he would need to complete the project he was working on. He had hoped to be finished in time to go on the trip, but he had no way of estimating.

Steve told Connie from the beginning that he felt like the outing would add too much to their already full life and maybe it wasn't a good idea at this time. Connie was so excited about the thought of visiting her friends that she didn't hear him. All she knew was that she really wanted to go; it was important to her and their friends were counting on their visit.

Steve felt under pressure from Connie, who was determined to go on this excursion. She was not listening to his appeal to remain open and see whether or not it would be possible. Would he finish in time, would he be too tired considering all that he was committed to do?

Steve saw the importance of staying in the moment and was trying not to jump ahead with a premature decision, but there was no support from his wife to wait and see. What he didn't know was that his indecision of whether to go or not had nothing to do with the discomfort that he was experiencing.

Finally, one morning, as the date to leave was getting closer and Steve was not finished with his job and Connie was still determined to go, he became extremely frustrated. He accepted his frustration, confusion, and anger with his wife. And then the insight came. The pressure of making a decision was gone. It was now clear to him that the decision was not the point; none of the conflict had anything to do with the trip at all. It was all about their habit of not staying in the moment.

This scenario was a familiar habit that they often repeated in their relationship. Connie was prone to making plans that included Steve without always listening deeply to his response. In her excitement about the plans she never noticed that she was not considering his true feelings. She assumed that they were in agreement because she didn't hear an ultimate "no." Her focus was on her plans rather than living in the moment. She never noticed that she had closed the door to heart-to-heart communication. Steve sensed her resistance when he tried to bring up the subject and felt pressured to make a decision about the situation. He responded to the pressure by thinking that making the decision would solve the problem. They were both looking at the details and missing the solution.

Later that day Connie brought up the trip and asked if he had made a decision. She was trying not to apply pressure, but he could sense her uneasiness about the outcome. Now Steve could answer clearly and with resolve. He told her from his heart without judgment that they didn't need to decide whether or not they were going to Chicago, they needed to decide if they were going to live in the moment.

Steve lovingly showed her that before, when he brought up his concerns about the trip, she had not responded from trust in a benevolent spiritual universe but from fear of not having her expectations met. Connie had become caught up in the details and was attempting to force a decision when unknown factors were not in place. He too had been caught up in the details by trying to make a premature decision.

Steve and Connie looked at their habit and saw that their solution was to remember that no matter what the details are, to stay in the moment and they would see what to do. He assured her that he would like to go to Chicago if the timing worked out. They saw how they might move their plans forward one day to increase the chance of him finishing his project and resting.

When awareness of our true Self is clouded, so is our thinking. The stage is set for conflict and disagreement. If conflicts arise, it's a signal to be open and to allow balance to return. Fortunately, we have the ability within our true Self to become aware of our habits and to transform them into opportunities that take us to a deeper level of awareness in our relationship.

Connie and Steve found a wholehearted resolution. They were in total agreement that following the guidance of their spiritual nature was their true intention. Little did they know at the onset that what seemed to be about a trip to Chicago turned out to be a solid commitment to living their lives in the powerful present moment.

In the wholehearted model, the natural Self responds from love rather than fear. In timeless love, there is no conflict, only harmony. We realize that conflict is merely limited thinking that comes from the illusion that we are separate. Fortunately, we have the power of awareness and the freedom to return to our natural Self, which provides us with insights that result in harmony. We know that we are not separate; we are joined in spirit. We only appear to be separate because we are individual expressions of divine love.

The wholehearted model may sound unrealistic and naive, but it is the most powerful and practical solution to conflict in any relationship. It is the only method that can create a true meeting of the minds and hearts. In the following diagram, we see that our differences can be transcended by a flash of insight (new thinking) that results in a wholehearted resolution.

Just considering the possibility of wholehearted resolution makes us feel hopeful.

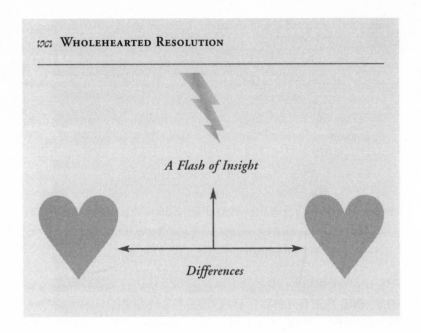

### ⚡ Wholehearted Resolution

*A Flash of Insight*

*Differences*

Wholehearted resolution innately contains the following ingredients. I composed the following list of ingredients to remind you of what naturally exists between two people operating from wholeheartedness. This list will give you a reference point should you slip out of timeless love and into the time-bound habits of your belief system.

- Willingness
- Deep listening
- Presence
- Letting go of the ego-self and choosing the natural Self
- Recognizing the source of experience and separate realities
- Forgiveness
- Heart-to-heart communication

I will only go into depth on willingness, the first ingredient; I have already covered the other ingredients earlier in the book.

## *Willingness*

Willingness is the first and most important requirement for a wholehearted resolution. It is faith and humility in action that assumes that an answer or solution will appear if we are open to it. It demonstrates a knowing that there is a greater intelligence than that contained in our small, ego-based intellect. Willingness unblocks the dam in our ego-based thinking and opens up the possibility for our level of understanding to rise.

Because fear keeps us from timeless love, it is a barrier to using the wholehearted resolution model. Innocently, we have been unwilling to give up our fears and the realities we have constructed to protect us from our fears. We hold our love and ourselves separate from the world and/or our partner to protect ourselves. But our natural Self, the truth, and timeless love have no need for protection.

We all have the innate desire to love and to be loved. All we need is the willingness to follow that innate desire. If we withhold our love and the full expressions of our spiritual nature, we not only keep it from our partner and everyone else, but we also keep it from ourselves. Simply stated, giving and receiving are one. We can only receive what we are willing to give.

In so many conflicts in the world, at an individual and a global level, an impasse always occurs when there is a lack of willingness to look within for solutions. When we rigidly hold on to our present beliefs about a situation, this viewpoint blinds us to any new answers that may be suggested. If the alternative answers are inconsistent with our ego-beliefs, we will cast aside these new possibilities. In this way we are innocently caught in the loop of our ego's thought system and a solution is nonexistent at that level of consciousness. Willingness is the key that removes the dam and allows all the other ingredients in the whole-hearted resolution model to flow. This process opens us up to listening to our heart and allowing us to access our natural Selves.

The following story illustrates the wholehearted resolution model. It demonstrates the possibility of turning a potential conflict into an opportunity for transforming our relationships and ourselves.

### The Wake-Up Call

Frank and Joan were successful and positive and were admired by many people for their commitment to family, to each other, and to helping those in need. Though their life was very much in the fast lane, they valued spirituality and the concept of a slower-paced life.

Frank, a psychologist, was one of the most energetic people I have ever met. I would call him "Mr. Enthusiasm." He was very upbeat about everything in his life. He deeply loved and admired his children and would do anything for them; he always attended to his psychotherapy patients and loved them like family; and he was very active in his church, his community, his fishing club, Boy Scouts, and numerous other social activities. However, many issues in his marriage with Joan were never dealt with because of the fast pace of their lives—among them were financial irresponsibility, overconsumption, and lack of time for intimacy and quality communication.

Over the years, Joan tried to turn Frank's attention to all these issues. For a while he would sincerely attempt to change, but before long he was back into his old habits of distraction, busy-mindedness, workaholism, and not listening. Joan was loyal to Frank but began to escape through her own activities and also through food. On some level, she had begun to give up on ever rekindling intimacy with Frank.

A few years ago, Frank learned about Health Realization. To his credit he was very open and willing to change his entire approach to counseling, even though he was already very successful and respected by his colleagues. He did start to slow down dramatically, but it was not nearly enough.

One spring, Frank started to feel sluggish. This was highly unlike him, as he was used to working and playing equally hard sixteen to eighteen hours a day. He consulted his physician and was put through a series of tests. Frank's brother had died of liver cancer at a young age, and this thought kept lurking in the minds of both Frank and Joan.

Finally, after no diagnosis was apparent, the doctors decided to do an MRI and other more extensive tests. Though the results were negative, Frank's doctor told him and Joan that he believed there was a 95 percent chance that Frank had pancreatic cancer, and the doctor recommended a drastic and invasive surgery that would require a three-month recovery period.

The couple was shocked, speechless, and near panic. "How could this be true?" Frank pleaded with the doctor. "I have so much more living to do. I thought the other tests had said there was no cancer."

The doctor put his hand on Frank's shoulder. "If my wife were in your shoes, I would do this surgery on her. I care deeply for you, Frank. You are a good friend and I know this could save your life." Frank trusted his doctor totally and knew that his doctor cared for him, yet he and Joan still put off this drastic remedy for a couple of weeks while they sought other opinions. Everyone came back with the same recommendation: that surgery was required as soon as possible.

Frank and Joan felt horrified at all the implications of this shocking news. They would have to get all their finances together if Frank were to be out of work so long. They would have to update their wills. All the things they had put off doing in their busy lives suddenly hit them between the eyes. They weren't prepared for this event financially or emotionally. This crisis was a painful and frightening wake-up call for both of them.

They could no longer deny the financial tightrope they were on. Everything they usually thought was absolutely necessary—their social commitments and work—would have to be put on hold. Most important, they could no longer put their relationship on the back burner.

These insights, as painful as they were, were really what both of them already knew at the level of their true Selves. All the issues, problems, and conflicts were an illusionary creation of their ego-selves. When they woke up to the reality of their situation they allowed the truth to come to the surface. The shock of Frank's illness, surgery, long recovery period, and potential death made them come to their senses and return to their spiritual core. They saw what was truly important for both of them as a couple.

Their lives became an emotional roller coaster for the next six weeks, and they alternated between insecurity and a deep sense of calm. They reached out to friends and family for love and support. And they sought counsel from people with a depth of understanding that would point them in the direction of equanimity, rather than panic and fear. They knew they couldn't do it alone, and they needed reminders that they could return to a place of love and peace.

Frank and Joan came away from this true-life crisis better than they went into it. They are now full of gratitude for life itself, for each other, and for the love of family and friends, the depth of which they had no idea before this crisis occurred. Rather than being victims of life's unfairness, they humbly accepted their fate and opened themselves up to growth and insights. In essence, they became willing. Their willingness has opened the door to new illuminations about timeless love.

They returned to wholeheartedness. Included in this higher level of consciousness were the qualities of listening deeply, quieting their minds, acceptance, many heart-to-heart talks, forgiveness, knowing the source of their experience, the importance of presence with each other, reaching out to others for support, and living from a deep sense of faith. They believed that somehow it would all work out, whatever the outcome. Out of the intelligence of their deeper wisdom came appropriate new habits: they quit watching TV and turning to other forms of distraction. They made a priority for meditation and prayer, and took time to be with each other and friends. This health crisis caused them to wake up to what was really important in their lives and helped them reclaim their powerful natural Selves.

They shared with me that through this apparent adversity, they could see major changes that needed to take place in their lives and in their relationship. By staying wholehearted and connected to their spiritual core, they were guided to implement the following three changes.

LESSON 1: THEY BECAME MORE RESPONSIBLE The first thing they had to do after the meeting with the doctor was to meet with their banker to see how they would finance Frank's medical costs and period of convalescence with no income for three months. As they went through their monthly expenses and all their overhead, Frank realized what Joan had been trying to tell him for years—they were living beyond their means. He was shocked. Initially, this realization was as dramatic to him as the news of the possibility of cancer. They had to take out a home improvement loan to live on for a few months and started making plans to sell their house and downsize their lifestyle. Frank and Joan had many heartfelt discussions that led to greater honesty between them. They realized how they had put material things ahead of a lifestyle that would leave time for intimacy and quiet reflection. As a result, they were always staying one step ahead of the bill collectors. Frank said he realized that "Life isn't about having and getting, it's about being and becoming."

LESSON 2: THEY LEARNED TO SLOW DOWN AND EXPERIENCE THE RICHNESS OF QUIET As I said earlier, Frank and Joan were in life's fast lane—chasing after success and acquisitions. As Frank was forced to rest most of the time and was bedridden for two months, his mind began to slow down. He and Joan spent many quiet moments together doing nothing but being together. They had never done this before. They went from believing and preaching about slowing down to actually living it.

**LESSON 3: THEIR LIVES FILLED WITH LOVE AND INTIMACY**
"We watched an unfolding and blossoming of our family and friendships," said Frank. "We were stunned at the outpouring of love and support from all our kids and our friends. We moved from financial richness to spiritual richness as a couple." Frank and Joan were awakened by this health crisis in their lives to find that they had so much more than they ever realized. By staying wholehearted and rejoining their natural Selves, they rose above the level of fear. What in the beginning had been a crisis was now a gift, as they reached a new wholehearted level of awareness. They understood that blessings were all around them and in them, which their fast-paced life had masked. The love and intimacy that had been out of reach was now there for them to reclaim as they began to live in the wholeness of their natural Selves.

Frank recovered and he and Joan transcended this major crisis in their lives by facing it with willingness and faith. They surrendered to the unknown, filled with love rather than with the sense of fear that had previously and unknowingly driven their lives.

# The Whole Is Greater Than the Sum of Its Parts

The power of sharing with each other from a wholehearted place cannot be overstated. When Frank and Joan embraced each other in timeless love, they became one with Universal Love—the source of all things—and had the cooperation and intelligence of it available to them. When we join together in timeless love, we are held within the oneness of the Spirit in return. Wholeheartedness brings the power of Divine Love to our aid. At this level of awareness, Frank and Joan could see beyond problems and solutions to the inner knowing of who they were and what to do next in their lives.

Even though we may not be able to stay wholehearted throughout all of our heart-to-heart discussions, the moments we remain authentic give profound meaning to our relationships. These moments reunite us with each other and the whole—which is greater than the sum of its parts.

In the next chapter, we will look at ways of becoming love and the future of love and relationships in our world. I will show how all the principles and guidelines to timeless love can actually change the future of intimate relationships.

# 10

# BECOMING LOVE

*The moon is complete, its slivers are illusions; eclipsed by the world, we await illumination.*

—MICHAEL BAILEY

LAST SUMMER, our friend's daughter got married. He has been a teacher and therapist of Health Realization for many years and his daughter, Julia, was raised in a home where the principles taught in this book were lived. I was always struck by her joyful nature and by the wisdom of her youth, but at her wedding I was bowled over with the power of the love she and her new husband shared. I don't know if I ever experienced that much love at a wedding. Jacob and Julia radiated presence, joy, and all the attributes of love we have spoken of. As a result of experiencing their wedding, I knew I had to write this chapter. I wanted to express what is possible for the future of relationships that are based on this understanding—the unlimited potential that awaits us all. I wanted to write of becoming love.

Finding timeless love is a process of becoming love. It is within your reach and requires acceptance of where you are now. At times, you may find that you are in your ego-self, reacting and seemingly back where you started. Don't judge yourself; it is part of the process to go in and out of awareness of your natural Self. Becoming love is a commitment to discovering your true Self and the feelings of love and having total faith in the wisdom of your true feelings. As I said in Chapter 1, we are love, and discovering the truth of this is the process.

Here is the story of how Julia and Jacob got through the first phases of their relationship and how this experience set the tone for their marriage.

### Bumbling Through Love

Like Julia, Jacob had been exposed to the principles of Health Realization in many seminars. Actually, he and Julia met at one of those sessions. They were immediately attracted to each other and started communicating by E-mail, as she was living in Hawaii and he in Portland. A few months after they met, he visited her in Hawaii and they realized they were in love. However, Julia also had a lot of judgments about Jacob and all the things that bugged her about him—the way he splashed on his aftershave lotion, and that he was nine years older, had some gray hair, and was divorced.

One day, he asked her how she was feeling about the relationship, and she expressed all those judgments and details with great emotion. Jacob didn't react, he didn't take any of it personally, he just listened and lovingly accepted her. Jacob's ability to respond to her in that manner neutralized her wrath. It is what transformed her judgments into appreciation for all his qualities. Thus began a pattern in their relationship of honesty, expression of emotions and true feelings, and acceptance.

When I asked them to elaborate on this pattern, Jacob said, "Every time we are honest, we are careful not to take what each other says personally. We just listen deeply to each other and our relationship grows more intimate. All the issues we make up in our thinking become transformed through this process. We grow closer each time we go through one of these heart-to-hearts."

Julia further shared, "I think that my initial insecurity about our age difference colored the way I saw him, and I would judge any little thing—I even thought the sandals he wore were ugly. Why couldn't he wear flip-flops like everyone else in Hawaii! These judgments disappeared when my insecurity faded. I realized that I only judge Jacob when I am in an insecure state. After this initial insecure stage, we would drop into long periods of timeless love, where we would stay up all night talking and sharing. Before we knew it, we were deeply in love, and I decided to move to Portland.

"Then, Jacob's insecurities really kicked in. He thought we were moving too fast and got scared. In his heart he knew we were right for each other, but his insecure thoughts and beliefs, coupled with the unsolicited advice of friends, caused him to question the timing of our moving in together."

"Julia was great," Jacob said. "She didn't take any of this personally. She knew it was right, and she knew I knew it. She could see that I was just temporarily caught up in my thinking. By not reacting to me and by accepting my struggling through this stage, Julia allowed me the room to change.

"I thought I had to be perfect before I committed to Julia. Through her acceptance of me, I realized that we would always be growing and changing, that we didn't have to be perfect before we committed to each other. We never would have gotten through this if Julia had taken all this personally. She gave me the room to bumble through this phase and be a mess for a while. We can get through this process; we don't have to have it all figured out before we commit and move forward. All we needed was love, trust, and acceptance."

Jacob's point about the acceptance of their bumbling is bigger than it seems. Acceptance of our humanity is acceptance that we are all in the process of becoming love—we are all going through different phases of realizing our perfection. Through love and acceptance, we move through our difficult times with each other.

## Awaiting Illumination

At the beginning of this chapter, I quoted from a short poem that is written on one of Michael's mixed-media paintings, titled *Phases I*, which looks like the moon in its phases. This very powerful piece illustrates seven phases of the moon, from a full moon to just a sliver. In reality, the moon is always complete, despite how it appears to our eyes. Our world blocks the view of its totality much of the time by casting a shadow of our earth on it. In the same way, we are always complete, yet we experience our true Selves in phases. These phases are the phases of becoming who we already are. In the previous story, Julia and Jacob's approach of acceptance and expression of themselves and their experience in every phase of their relationship allowed them to see more of the wholeness of their love.

The first part of the poem on the painting, "The moon is complete," symbolizes our completeness, our wholeness. We have talked about this wholeness as the true or natural Self or our spiritual nature.

"Eclipsed by the world" refers to how we look outside ourselves for happiness and love and thus get caught up in false images of our world and our ego-selves. We forget that the moon is always there in its totality by seeing only our perception of its incompleteness. In our relationships, we fall in love with the natural Self of each other. As time goes on, we begin to cast our shadows on each other, and thus we eclipse the true picture of our partner and ourselves. We misperceive this as falling out of love, but all it means is that we have momentarily seen our partner through the eyes of illusion or separation. When Julia didn't take Jacob's insecurity about moving in together personally, she was seeing his true Self and not taking his ego insecurities as who he really was. Many couples erroneously think that when the shadow of insecurity appears, they are finally seeing the true colors of their mate.

"We await illumination" is the last line in the poem. Illumination reveals itself when the shadow of the personal world of the ego recedes. Love is revealed in its full light. It is always there; we just don't see it when we focus on the shadow instead of the light. In our time-bound lives, we often lose presence and when we do, we cast the shadow of preoccupation and distraction onto our reality. We no longer feel connected to what is truly real—our natural Self—but still we await transformation. We wait for love to return. We are all looking for timeless love, whether we know it or not.

I will share a bit more of Julia and Jacob's story, in which they talk about the importance of presence in their relationship to bring them back to seeing their love.

### Committed to Connection

Julia: "When one of us is going through a hard time and is wrapped up in his or her thoughts a lot, the other will say, 'I miss you, come back.' That means to come back to where our hearts connect. When you know that when you are gone, not present, that the other person is waiting there with love and acceptance, it makes it easy to come back. Like the other day, Jacob had just gotten back from a two-day business trip, and we were sitting on the couch watching a movie. He was still thinking about his day and I said, 'I miss you.' He immediately came back to the present and we connected. Each time we reconnect, our love grows even deeper. We are committed to make always staying connected, no matter what, a priority."

Jacob: "We both get off track sometimes and caught up in our think-ing. When we do, we get easily annoyed and take things personally. When we don't feel good, our thinking isn't good either. We made a commitment that our priority is to be connected. We will often look at each other and laugh when we are "off," because we know at some point we will feel con-nected again, that it's just a phase. That really takes the pressure off. There is no urgency when we don't feel close, because we know it is temporary. By knowing that, we can accept our moments of being off, and they don't grow to days and weeks of being disconnected.

"So often, when we are down we feel an urgency to 'fix' things and talk it out, but we know that would be really bad timing. Knowing that our spirits will lift again helps us to just accept being down at that moment. Then we don't make things worse by trying to fix them when our think-ing is so off. It's helpful to know deep down inside that things are going to work out eventually, so you can back off. It lets the muddy water settle till you can see clearly again."

What does it mean to stay connected? Certainly, one definition is to feel a sense of sharing with each other, but true connectedness comes when each of us reunites with the true Self first. Then we can respond to each other from our illuminated spiritual nature. The commitment to rediscover and stay aligned with our spiritual, natural Self is the essence of becoming love.

## Commitment to the Discovery of the True Self

Michael and I celebrate our twentieth year of marriage next month. We have remained deeply committed to each other throughout that time, though we have had challenging detours along the way. The rud-der of our relationship has been our resolve to discover our true

Selves—our spiritual path that has led to expanding self-awareness, happiness, and an ever-deepening intimacy. As I look back on our lives together, I see how innocent we were at each phase of deepening awareness of our natural Selves. We were always doing the best we could at our level of understanding at the time. In hindsight, I see there was always more awareness of our spiritual Selves available. Until we became more conscious we couldn't imagine what it would be like to live in that awareness. Yet, each step of the way was special, and I always had the feeling that "certainly, it can't get any better than this." But it does.

Michael created a second mixed-media painting called *Phases II*. Similar to *Phases I* in design, *Phases II* has seven jewel-like glass sculptures mounted in a row in the painting instead of seven moon shapes from sliver to full. Each jewel, unique within itself, represents a phase on the path of becoming who we really are—our spiritual nature. In her poetry about the piece, she draws a parallel to the true Self by suggesting that each phase of becoming love is like a jewel in our crown. Each phase is an experience and discovery of an aspect of our spiritual Self. Like a hologram, within each aspect of our natural Self is contained the spiritual whole.

On our relationship journeys, we often negatively judge the phase we are currently in, or the phase our partner is currently in, or we erroneously think, as I have done, that our relationship is as strong as it can possibly be and it can't grow any further. If we accept each phase in its inherent perfection without seeing it as good or bad or best or worst, we will see its jewel. If we judge where we are or where our partner is, we will get stuck in the ego-self, which is always trying to "fix" what isn't broken. Some phases of my marriage to Michael were like the full bloom of spring; others were like the stillness and gestation of winter, but they were all necessary and beautiful as part of the unfolding of the inner wholeness that is already complete, like the moon.

One haiku says it very well: "The Spring comes, and the grass grows by itself." All the trying to improve ourselves and our relationships that we do, all the striving to become perfect—are all in vain. We are already complete and only await the shadow to recede and illumination to reveal that completion. What we fall in love with is the natural Self of each other, which is already complete. The process of becoming love is the process of remembering who we are and who our partner is. By accepting the jewel of each phase, we become love—our true, complete nature. I make it sound simple, and it is. However, if we lose sight of the commitment to discovery of our spiritual core, we lose our way very easily.

Throughout the past twenty-two years of our relationship, Michael's and my commitment to the discovery of our natural Selves has kept our love growing and becoming full. At times it has been difficult to keep my faith, because when I was in a low mood, our relationship didn't look complete—it looked wounded, tattered, and broken. It was only my attachment to my ego-belief system that created this illusion. Whenever I returned to the path of discovery, I found hope, and beauty, and love. I always reflected later on those times and thought, "How could I have ever doubted our love?" It is always so clear when I am clear.

It is my hope that all of you who read these words will be given the hope to continue on your journey of becoming love, because it is inevitable that you will become who you truly are. And, in so doing, you will find it with each other and with all of life.

# 11

# LOVE LETTERS

THIS CLOSING CHAPTER is meant to inspire you. It contains the love letters of some of the couples in this book who have shared their journeys of becoming love. I asked them to write the letters to you, the reader, or to each other and share them with you. Enjoy!

*Dear Rick,*

*I used to think that I knew where our relationship was going—the ups and downs and the feeling of getting through the tough times. But now I realize that I could never wholeheartedly predict where we will find ourselves today, tomorrow, next year, or years from now. I smile inside when you tell me you want to spend our retired years taking a walk together each morning. I picture us holding hands and walking in love.*

*The reason I can't predict the future of our relationship is because as soon as I feel our relationship is great, it gets better. And as soon as it gets better* than great, it gets better again. I could never imagine in my wildest dreams how wonderful it feels to be in love with another human being and able to share time on this earth together.

Sure, we get temporarily lost sometimes and get caught up in the obstacles of life. But now we are armed with the ability to see and understand one another from a deeper place. We are able to help one another and provide compassion when life takes turns that are troublesome and unexpected. We are strong together because we have an understanding of how we create our own experience from the inside out and from moment to moment. This understanding deepens our love, compassion, and mutual respect.

I used to think that I needed "things" to be happy—a bigger kitchen, a new house, a new car, another baby, or to fit into size-6 jeans. But now I see so clearly that my happiness comes from within. The most peaceful, sublime happiness I have ever experienced comes from within and is found in the space between my thoughts of "needing things."

Our relationship grows deeper, and being able to share, from moment-to-moment, the underlying feeling of love, illuminates our love for one another. With this understanding I am able to realize that this underlying feeling of love is always present and real. I am able to understand that to receive your love, I need to be in a healthy place. A busy head, a long to-do list, errands, household chores, and a frenetic pace used to take me away from receiving your love. Now I know I have a choice to create a busy mind and become preoccupied with life's routines or complete these routines in a state of calm that is open to receiving your love. It was simply that I had to get out of my own way, step aside, and let love bubble up from within. For example, I can't reach out to hold your hand if I'm not in a place to feel love, and yet the love is always present if I quiet down and I get out of my own way. It is a miracle to have gained this insight.

Gaining understanding comes in little pieces, and as the pieces fit together the puzzle becomes solved. As we reach deeper levels of understanding, our lives become enriched and we are able to see the big picture, the whole puzzle.

*I know in my heart that our relationship will continue to grow deeper as we become wiser. I can't wait to discover what is in store for us—each new discovery is beautifully wonderful.*

*Here's to living from the heart!*

*Love, Pamela*

### Dear Friends,

*What do I know about love today? I do know that my understanding of love is very different now from when I got married more than twenty years ago. What accounts for the change? It is a deep sense of gratitude that comes from understanding the true meaning and possibility of love. I don't see limits on this kind of love, but for now, let's look at the love we share and have for a partner. For me, that is my husband, Mark. Mark and I were friends before we were lovers. We enjoyed our time together, had similar interests, and ended up, by Supreme design, getting married. We always had a strong marriage that looked like everyone else's, in the two-cute-kids, two-good-careers, and go-to-church-on-Sunday model.*

*Was our love deep and meaningful and the best it could be? No, but did we know that or even imagine that there could be something else? No, so all is well until we hear about the unlimited possibilities found in the understanding called Health Realization. So, what did we hear? We learned that bother and irritation about another person's behavior is our own responsibility and generated by our own thinking. We learned that all people we meet live in a separate reality that is neither right nor wrong. And we learned that two souls and hearts can connect on a level so deep that a bond will be formed that will transcend time, trouble, and life. We found the gift of love!*

*A gift so profound, yet ordinary, that it manifests itself countless times every day. By listening deeply from a place filled with love, I open myself, in the pres-*

ence of another person, to unlimited possibilities of love in action. The ultimate human connection comes from hearts touching in a moment of freeflowing openness led by a calm, clear mind open to receiving and being touched by the heart of another human being.

This profound and moving experience, one we've all been searching for, is possible at any given moment in any given setting with any given person or persons. Although it feels magical, mystical, and out of the ordinary, it is not! It is a human birthright, a gift bestowed on us by a wise, loving Creator who made it available to each and every one of us.

I encourage you to be open to the possibility that you too have this gift, an opportunity to have the deepest, most moving experience with another human being that you've ever had. Make a list of people you would like to have this encounter with, be curious, open, and watch it happen. Oh yes, remember to include on that list an encounter with an unknown person so deep it will touch you at the core of your heart.

Consider the possibility and look forward to days filled with deep love, connection, and meaning.

With deepest love and warmest wishes, Karla

### Dear Reader,

Before falling in love with my husband, my head ruled many aspects of my life. I was proud of my ability to imagine potential outcomes from a situation and play with scenarios to achieve my objectives. I spent much energy trying to analyze and manage interactions. And that was just at work!

In meeting my husband and embracing the principles Joe talks about in this book, I was able to soar beyond the boundaries that my mind could create. I was able to open my heart to the possibilities.

When my husband and I met, we brought very different lives to the relationship. He had been married and had three children. I had never married.

*We both looked outwardly very strong, yet we were both very sensitive and easily hurt. People used to find me intimidating, yet I knew I was an absolute puddle inside.*

*When we talked about our future, I could only create elaborate scenes where I would end up being hurt. His children wouldn't like me much less love me, I imagined. It would be uncomfortable dealing with his ex. I would feel left out at all the important family moments. His family would never accept me. He couldn't really love me. I was masterful at projecting the possibilities.*

*When we dealt with difficult issues, we'd both state our points. Then I would push and push, committed to being right. He would often respond by emotionally retreating and disengaging. This dance went on and on. We loved each other, but we didn't know how to change the steps.*

*Finally by embracing deep listening, we had major breakthroughs. As we began to really listen to each other, without anticipating what we would say next, without judging what was being said, each of us felt incredibly loved. We began to feel the joy that came from really connecting with someone. With that listening came trust; trust that each of us had the other's best interest at heart. That trust brought better listening and a wonderful new cycle was created.*

*As I set my creative scenario building aside, I allowed myself just to be surprised by what came next. And it has always, yes, always been better than I could imagine. Like the time I came home, slipping back into old patterns worrying that I would be a third wheel that evening with my husband and his son. I opened the door thinking about what I might do to avoid it all when my husband's son came running around the corner, yelled my name, and gave me a big smile and a big hug. We have only begun a very wonderful journey.*

*With love, Alice*

The following letter was written to the future children of this couple.

*Dear Children,*

*You will hear from the world about the difficulty of relationships, and about the high rate of marriages that end up in divorce. You will hear that marriage/intimate relationship is "hard work." That relationships are about work and sacrifice, about "working through issues," and "working things out."*

*I believe that this is misguided. And I believe it sets us up for failure and disappointment.*

*I don't believe it's about "hard work."*

*It's not about "work" or "working through issues" or "working things out."*

*Yes, love takes commitment—commitment to be true to ourselves; commitment to offer our partner the trust, freedom, and support to continue to learn and grow as an individual; and most importantly, it takes a commitment to always reopening our heart to each other, to reconnecting, and refinding the feeling of love and intimacy.*

*It's about letting go, letting our "personal stuff," our insecurities, go and to allow room in our hearts for the feeling of love, intimacy, and connectedness to return. It's about knowing deep down that nothing needs to be fixed, and that when the "clouds" (of our personal thoughts/feelings) pass, the feeling of love and intimacy will always return. It's about trust and faith.*

*It's about "choosing" to let go of our own personal "stuff" and choosing to reopen our hearts.*

*In relationships, we constantly have this "choice"—the choice to hold on to our own insecurities (the thoughts that make us feel small, angry, trapped), or to let go of the insecurity and let in the love and peace and connectedness (connectedness to our true Selves, to our partner, and to the world/nature/spirit/God) that is our natural state.*

*When we choose this, our relationships and our lives are transformed.*

*Love, Dad and Mom*

# RECOMMENDED READINGS AND WEBSITES

Bailey, Joseph. *The Serenity Principle: Finding Inner Peace in Recovery.* San Francisco: HarperCollins, 1990.

Bailey, Joseph. *Slowing Down to the Speed of Life* Tape Series. Available through website: speedoflove.net.

Bailey, Joseph. *The Speed Trap: How to Avoid the Frenzy of the Fast Lane.* San Francisco: HarperSanFrancisco, 1999.

Carlson, Richard. *Don't Sweat the Small Stuff—And It's All Small Stuff.* New York: Hyperion, 1997. dontsweat.com.

Carlson, Richard, and Kris Carlson. *Don't Sweat the Small Stuff in Love.* New York: Hyperion, 2000.

Carlson, Richard, and Joseph Bailey. *Slowing Down to the Speed of Life.* San Francisco: HarperSanFrancisco, 1997.

*The Impersonal Life.* Marina Del Rey, Calif.: DeVorss Publications, 1941, 1969.

Tolle, Eckhart. *The Power of Now.* Novato, Calif.: New World Library, 1999.

# INDEX